Southern Literary Studies
Fred Hobson, Editor

Self and Community in the Fiction of
ELIZABETH SPENCER

Self and Community in the Fiction of

ELIZABETH SPENCER

Terry Roberts

Louisiana State University Press / Baton Rouge and London

Designer: Amanda McDonald Key
Typeface: Bembo
Typesetter: Precision Typographers, Inc.
Printer and binder: Thomson–Shore, Inc.

Library of Congress Cataloging-in-Publication Data

Roberts, Terry, 1956–
    Self and community in the fiction of Elizabeth Spencer / Terry
Roberts.
        p.   cm. — (Southern literary studies)
    Includes bibliographical references and index.
    ISBN 0-8071-1879-6 (cloth)
    1. Spencer, Elizabeth—Criticism and interpretation.   2. Southern
States in literature.   3. Community life in literature.   4. Self in
literature.   I. Title.   II. Series.
PS3537.P4454Z85   1993
813'.54—dc20   93-26078
                                                     CIP

The author is grateful to Elizabeth Spencer for permission to quote from her novels *Fire in the Morning*, *This Crooked Way*, *The Voice at the Back Door*, *The Light in the Piazza*, *No Place for an Angel*, and *The Salt Line*; to the University Press of Mississippi for permission to quote from Elizabeth Spencer, *On the Gulf* and *The Snare*, and from Peggy Whitman Prenshaw, ed., *Conversations with Elizabeth Spencer*; to Doubleday, a division of Bantam, Doubleday, Dell Publishing Group, Inc., for permission to quote from *The Stories of Elizabeth Spencer* (1981); and to the editor of *Mississippi Quarterly* for permission to use material from Terry Roberts, "This Crooked Narrative Way," which appeared in Vol. XLVI (Winter, 1992–93), 61–75.

He thanks the publisher for permission to quote excerpts from *Jack of Diamonds and Other Stories*, by Elizabeth Spencer. Copyright © 1988 by Elizabeth Spencer. Used by permission of Viking Penguin, a division of Penguin Books USA Inc; and from *The Night Travellers*, by Elizabeth Spencer. Copyright © 1991 by Elizabeth Spencer. Used by permission of Viking Penguin, a division of Penguin Books USA Inc.

Lines from "Crazy Jane Talks with the Bishop" are reprinted with permission of Macmillan Publishing Company from *The Poems of W. B. Yeats: A New Edition*, edited by Richard J. Finneran. Copyright 1933 by Macmillan Publishing Company, renewed 1961 by Bertha Georgie Yeats.

Quotations are reprinted with permission of Twayne Publishers, an imprint of Macmillan Publishing Company, from *Elizabeth Spencer* by Peggy Whitman Prenshaw. Copyright © 1985 by G. K. Hall & Co.

For M.E.H.

Whose face I see in each moonrise,
Whose voice I hear in the river's run,
Whose touch is that of the cool night air,
And whose heart beats the pulse of the sun.

This idea . . . of "community" is a kind of ancient theme as well. The whole sort of mystical issue of just who your brothers and sisters really are. It occurs over and over again in religious writing. All the central characters in my stories do seem to have that problem— finding out where they belong . . . and who they belong with.

—Elizabeth Spencer

Contents

Preface

My purpose in writing this book has always been both to reopen Elizabeth Spencer's novels and stories for the scholarly community and at the same time to provide an adequate introduction for readers encountering some of her more difficult work for the first time. With the first goal in mind, I have organized this study chronologically in order to illustrate how the theme of community has affected Spencer's artistic growth. In line with the latter goal, I have tried to write each chapter as a coherent whole that can be used independently of the rest of the book. For all who use this study, I hope I have proven that while Spencer's artistic path has been occasionally misunderstood, it has led her and her readers into ever more complex and more satisfying literary creation.

There have been a number of scholars and friends who have helped in this endeavor. All Spencer students owe Peggy Whitman Prenshaw a bow for breaking first ground in Spencer studies with her typical wit and style. In addition, I personally owe a great deal to the Department of English of the University of North Carolina at Chapel Hill, including very specific debts to Doris Betts, Joe Flora, Robert Haig, Fred Hobson, and Linda Wagner-Martin, all of whom read early drafts of this study with sharp but friendly eyes. Robert Bain directed this project first as a dissertation, and what clarity there is in the prose was put there—often firmly—by him. When the manuscript went finally to LSU Press, first John Easterly and then Louis D. Rubin, Jr., were both encouraging and insightful. Those readers who know any or all of these scholars and editors need not be told that what grace and good sense there is here began with them. I myself added the nicks and dents.

Finally, there are two women without whom this study literally would not exist. They are the ones, after all, who have made this labor a very special one of love. If Elizabeth Spencer had not devoted her life to her art and then been both patient and honest in answering my questions, there would have been no ground to build on. If my wife were not just herself and no one else, then I could not, from day one, have dedicated all this work to her.

Self and Community in the Fiction of
ELIZABETH SPENCER

Introduction

Near the end of Elizabeth Spencer's third novel, *The Voice at the Back Door*, Duncan Harper, a white man, drives out into the countryside with his wife to pick up a black man named Beck Dozer. This simple scenario is complicated by the time, the early 1950s; the place, rural Mississippi; and the fact that the idealistic Harper is the interim sheriff of Winfield County running for the permanent post on an integrationist platform. He and his wife, Tinker, are driving out to pick up Dozer (who is accused of shooting a white bootlegger), not so much to prevent Dozer's escape as to prevent his lynching.

When Harper finds Dozer at an isolated country store, they are harassed by two white drifters, and the tension escalates to the point where Harper invites Dozer to *get into the front seat of the car beside him and his wife.* Nothing Duncan Harper has done to this point in the campaign is so dangerous. The threat of imminent violence is all but palpable, and in the only italicized passage in the novel, Harper realizes that "it comes to this. . . . To the tiniest decision you can make. To the slightest action. In front of people daring you to do what you believe in and they don't."[1] Harper is dead within minutes, probably because the drifters sabotaged his car.

What is so characteristically Spencerian about this scene is the nature of Harper's realization—that he and every other individual in Winfield County are bound up in a tangled web of community assumptions and beliefs. Even the slightest gesture causes public repercussions. Although this novel and particularly this scene concern an especially ugly and irrational aspect of southern community life, all of Spencer's characters, whether from the far North or the Deep South, eventually come to an epiphany similar to that of Duncan Harper. They all eventually come to recognize the subtle and pervasive power of community.

The relationship of the individual to the community has been Spencer's central concern since the beginning of her career. In her

---

1. Elizabeth Spencer, *The Voice at the Back Door* (New York, 1956), 300. Hereinafter cited by page number in the text.

early Mississippi novels, she focused on the confining social web of small southern towns. In the later, more cosmopolitan novels, she studied not only more complex social communities but also the inner lives of her characters as they are affected by communal life. Her interest in the pervasive problems faced by twentieth-century society led her naturally to focus on the interior lives of the disaffected and alienated—those who either rejected or were rejected by their native groups. This interest in the twentieth century's emotional vagabonds led in turn to a period of artistic experimentation, the result of which was the less accessible, less immediately popular novels of the 1960s and 1970s. Spencer has most successfully portrayed the alienated psyche in her three most recent novels, *The Snare, The Salt Line,* and *The Night Travellers,* which, for now at least, mark the culmination of her career.

Spencer's experiments in technique—primarily in narrative structure, point of view, and the use of external landmarks to mirror internal states of mind—were the direct result of her desire to explore her characters' inner lives in more depth than traditional narrative allowed. They grew out of her all-but-obsessive interest in how the individual both shapes and is shaped by the surrounding community. The steadily increasing appreciation paid Spencer's novels during the 1940s and 1950s may well have been due to the fact that they are so readily identifiable as "southern." They were obviously a part of a creative and critical tradition that was then and still is fascinated with the dynamics of community. Many of the writers and most of the canonized critics of southern literature have written on the subject, including Allen Tate, C. Hugh Holman, Lewis P. Simpson, Robert Penn Warren, and Louis D. Rubin, Jr.

The haunting of southern literary criticism by the idea of community is nowhere more evident than in Faulkner criticism. Faulkner's entire body of work concerns not only the mythical landscape of Yoknapatawpha County but also the overlapping communal webs of Native American, African American, poor white, and aristocratic gentry that populated that "postage stamp" of soil. In reaction, Faulkner scholars have emphasized the theme of community from the earliest (see Malcolm Cowley's 1944 introduction to *The Portable Faulkner*) to the most distinguished (read Cleanth Brooks, for example, on *Absalom, Absalom!*) to the very latest (John N. Duvall's monograph of 1990, *Faulkner's Marginal Couple: Invisible, Outlaw, and Unspeakable Communities*).

In Spencer's case, the scholars have not seen the same pervasiveness of this theme, but there are still fascinating parallels between Spencer's fiction and the body of traditional southern criticism. Allen Tate, whom Spencer first met in Italy in 1954, defined *communion* in "The Man of Letters in the Modern World" as a spiritual necessity, an echo of Spencer's use of the term in *The Snare*. Humanity, wrote Tate, has "got to communicate through love. Communication that is not also communion is incomplete. We *use* communication; we *participate* in communion."[2] Tate's fellow agrarian Robert Penn Warren was similarly fascinated with the human need for community, as evidenced both in his fiction (for example, the 1977 novel *A Place to Come To*) and in his criticism. He wrote of Conrad, for example, that his "characteristic story . . . becomes . . . the relation of man to the human community," and he describes Emilia Gould, a character in *Nostromo*, as sensitive to "the human community, the sense of human solidarity in understanding and warmth and kindness, outside the historical process."[3] This same concern runs as a thread through Warren's classic essays on Faulkner and Welty as well, suggesting that he, like his fellow southerner Tate, sees community and communion as central to human experience.

Perhaps the best reference point in classical southern criticism for Spencer's fiction, however, is one of the more recent statements—Louis Rubin's "From Combray to Ithaca: or, The 'Southernness' of Southern Literature" (1990), written after Rubin's four decades of reflection on things southern. "A work of Southern literature," Rubin explains, "is *Southern* not because it contains certain ingredients, whether those elements be language, subject matter, plot, characterization, or ideas, but because some or all of those elements have been made to take on attributes in relationship to one another that might not otherwise exist in just that way." The "catalyst" that defines southern literature, Rubin argues, "is the central importance of a community relationship." Furthermore, "what makes the oft-remarked Sense of Place in Southern fiction so important is the vividness, the ferocity even, with which it implies social and community attitudes."[4] This sense of "social and community attitudes," I

2. Allen Tate, "The Man of Letters in the Modern World," in Tate, *Collected Essays* (Denver, 1959), 385.

3. Robert Penn Warren, " 'The Great Mirage': Conrad and *Nostromo*," in Warren, *Selected Essays* (New York, 1951), 40, 36.

4. Louis D. Rubin, Jr., "From Combray to Ithaca: or, The 'Southernness' of Southern Literature," in Rubin, *The Mockingbird in the Gum Tree: A Literary Gallimaufry* (Baton Rouge, 1991), 22, 28, 33.

would maintain, defines Elizabeth Spencer's fiction throughout her career, not just in the early Mississippi novels.

After writing those early novels, however, Spencer changed artistic directions. She decided to focus her attention on the same emotional and psychological territory—communal life—but in a larger, more troubled world. The demands of both her thematic material and her imagination led her on to what she has since called "a certain path, a personal road."[5] In its earliest stages, this path crossed well-worn literary territory—that of backcountry Mississippi. Her focus on community was evident in each of her first three books, culminating in *The Voice at the Back Door* (1956). This novel has, instead of a single protagonist, a quadrangle of two men and two women that has a history, an evolving personality, and a fascinating self-consciousness. With this group of characters Spencer studies in depth the sort of painful definition of communal context that the characters in her more conventional southern novels undergo. In fact, the small towns in these novels prove so constricting that several important characters leave the South altogether for lonely lives elsewhere. When Spencer transferred the settings of her work from Mississippi to Italy, she began to examine more closely these characters who abandon home communities for lives as aliens.

Spencer's two Italian novellas, *The Light in the Piazza* and *Knights and Dragons*, illustrate clearly this change in artistic direction. The first is largely traditional in form and narration, more like the Mississippi books than the experimental novels that follow. In *Knights and Dragons*, however, Spencer shifts her narrative point of view more deeply inside her protagonist, Martha Ingram, studying her inner development at the expense of an externalized plot. Martha Ingram's tale is one of alienation and near madness, reflecting Spencer's growing interest in characters stripped of communal definition and support. However, even with Martha Ingram, the most solitary of her protagonists, Spencer emphasizes the individual's need for community. Although *Knights and Dragons* is not as finished a work as those that follow, Spencer's experiments with architecture and cityscape as mirrors for internal states of mind and her allegorical use of secondary characters signal a technical revolution in her work.

No Place for an Angel, the first major work to follow *Knights and*

5. Elizabeth Spencer, preface to *The Stories of Elizabeth Spencer* (Garden City, N.Y., 1981), xi.

Dragons, illustrates dramatically Spencer's willingness to mold narrative structure, chronology, and point of view to fit her thematic material—in this case, the rootless nihilism of postwar American culture. In this amoral culture, the worst characters are ruthlessly efficient and the best crippled by their own ennui. All are sensitive to their lost hold on the identity created by communal context, but none knows how to return to a meaningful life.

In *The Snare*, Spencer portrays a young woman who rejects the best New Orleans society has to offer for "the crooked life." The protagonist of the novel, Julia Garrett, trades the benefits of wealth and status for the thrill and passion of jazz musicians, drugs, and the lurking power of the underworld. The message of *The Snare* is that the individual psyche seeks in the community at large corruption as well as love, violence as well as healing.

Julia Garrett is also a significant character in Spencer's artistic growth because with her, Spencer solves the problem that had haunted her work since *Knights and Dragons*. Her emphasis on the interior lives of her characters had created a less accessible fiction, a fiction that sometimes lacked the suspenseful external reality of her earlier novels. In *The Snare*, however, Spencer resolves the dilemma by returning to her original obsession with the relationship between individual and community. "What I hoped would happen," she has said of the novel, "is that the reader would catch the connection between Julia and the city and so read it as an exploration, in depth, of both simultaneously. . . . New Orleans reveals the woman and the woman reveals New Orleans."[6]

By the time she wrote *The Snare*, Spencer had begun to reimagine the South, re-creating it as a fictional landscape. Having developed her narrative range in *Knights and Dragons* and *No Place for an Angel*, she was able to combine the portrait of her protagonist with the portrait of New Orleans. Appropriately, this artistic reconciliation occurs in a novel about spiritual reconciliation; through her harrowing experiences in the New Orleans underworld, Julia Garrett discovers the value of *communion*, the spiritual breaking of bread among equals, the symbolic sharing of lives. Her spiritual recovery foreshadows the new tone of reconciliation that characterizes Spencer's work since the mid-1970s. Having rejected her parents' reli-

6. Terry Roberts, "A Whole Personality: Elizabeth Spencer," in *Conversations with Elizabeth Spencer*, ed. Peggy Whitman Prenshaw (Jackson, 1991), 228.

gious fundamentalism as a child (see her story "A Christian Education," 1974), she began to write about the South again in the 1970s with a new and quite different spirituality. Although there are supernatural elements in her early stories, there is a burgeoning of the mystical in her later fiction, most notably in response to the Gulf coast. In returning to Julia Garrett's New Orleans (in *The Snare*) and then later to Arnie Carrington's Gulf coast (in *The Salt Line*), Spencer is returning not to the same rural Mississippi of her earliest work but to a southern landscape she has reimagined for her own artistic purposes. The coast in particular is a magical landscape where visions occur and where "the one chance in infinity" that anything has "of going right" is most likely to materialize.[7]

This new mood of reconciliation that characterizes the stories and novels of the 1970s and 1980s is an organic part of Spencer's mastery of the techniques with which she had experimented since *Knights and Dragons*. Nowhere is this mastery more evident than in *The Salt Line*. In this magical novel she uses a shifting point of view, a uniquely tidal structure, and a series of powerful images to study the rebirth and growth of a community. Here, as in Shakespeare's *Tempest*, which the novel echoes, communal relations are treated as profoundly sacred. And in retrospect, it would seem that it is to this conclusion that Spencer has all along been leading us—in its deepest sense *community* equals *communion*, with all its spiritual connotations.

Thus, when readers trace Spencer's career from the early popular novels to the present, they discover steadily increasing technical sophistication coupled with richer and more intricate studies of community. While her best-known novels, *The Voice at the Back Door* and *The Light in the Piazza*, have received well-deserved attention, her more challenging, more sophisticated fiction has been generally ignored or misread. *This Crooked Way* and the less accessible, more experimental novels published after 1975 successfully convey a deeper, more complex view of the world and deserve both joyful rereading and enlightened reevaluation.

7. Elizabeth Spencer, *The Salt Line* (Garden City, N.Y., 1984), 299. Hereinafter cited by page number in the text.

1 / *Feuding Families*

I don't think most Southerners of even the recent generations have lost the deep-seated sense of home. . . . If you live in a place until you're six years old, you belong to it.

—Elizabeth Spencer, in an interview

Elizabeth Spencer's fascination with community dynamics is obvious even in her first novel, *Fire in the Morning*. Published in 1948 and one of her three "Mississippi novels," it is concerns the painful resolution of a thirty-five-year feud between two prominent families in a small Mississippi town. As stereotypical, even hackneyed, a topic as this may now seem, *Fire in the Morning* is in at least one respect quite unlike its southern forebears.[1] The novel does not focus on the development of individual characters. In fact, with only a few exceptions, the characters seem quite one-dimensional. Instead Spencer describes in detail the relationships between people, the ties that bind them together. As Herbert Creekmore perceptively wrote of *Fire in the Morning*, "It is not so much a study of the character or people (a misconception fostered by always thinking 'hero-heroine') as of the character of a complex of people—the moral relationship of the citizens of a community."[2] Spencer portrays communities within communities here—notably marriages within families within the larger "complex" of Tarsus itself.

Although Spencer's narrative method in *Fire in the Morning* is relatively traditional, she foreshadows in this first novel the same

1. As Peggy Prenshaw notes, reviewers found echoes of Faulkner, Warren, and Lillian Hellman. Prenshaw, *Elizabeth Spencer* (Boston, 1985), 16.
2. Herbert Creekmore, "Submerged Antagonisms," *New York Times Book Review*, September 12, 1948, P. 16.

concerns she will treat with more sophistication later in her career. She will in later novels expand the focus on traditional marriages to include intimate groups of three or more individuals. She will also focus her study of extended groups on the internal impact they have on individuals rather than on their external melodrama. As these themes become more complex, Spencer will use a series of experiments—multiple narrators, shifts in time and point of view, imagery used to control development—to capture precisely the fictional medium that mirrors her message. *Fire in the Morning*, in other words, inaugurates a series of efforts on Spencer's part to portray the dynamics of communal existence, internal as well as external.

If it is fair to say in this context that the novel has a protagonist, it is Kinloch Armstrong, the son of a widely admired farmer and former sheriff, Daniel Armstrong. The aptly named Kinloch (trapped within his family and community in ways he does not understand) has since childhood instinctively disliked the wealthiest family in Tarsus, the Gerrards. During the course of the novel Kinloch discovers the past outrages that sparked the feud between the Armstrongs and the Gerrards, and more significantly, he also discovers the many ties that bind them together. Spencer portrays Kinloch Armstrong realizing his own human frailty as well as the humanity of the Gerrards. In facing the moral complexity of his and his family's history, he sees that, as his father says, "You cannot hate a man, you cannot kill a man because of his last name."[3]

Even in writing about Kinloch's growth as a character, Spencer focuses on the interwoven communities in which it occurs. His antipathy for the Gerrards becomes a factor in his troubled relationships to his wife, father, and cousin, and, ultimately, to the community of Tarsus.[4] Although Spencer sets her stage with an ongoing feud in a dusty southern town, the significant action occurs on three other levels: within the characters' families, especially within their marriages, and finally within the community consciousness. The psychological pressures created by the unresolved feud and the entrance of certain outsiders into the community precipitate drastic change in all three arenas.

*　　*　　*

3. Elizabeth Spencer, *Fire in the Morning* (New York, 1948), 148. Hereinafter cited by page number in the text.

4. Prenshaw points out Kinloch's resemblance to the biblical Saul of Tarsus, who also "makes an arduous journey of the spirit." Prenshaw, *Elizabeth Spencer*, 17.

The two contentious families in the novel are the Gerrards—notably the powerful Simon Gerrard, his son Lance, his daughter Justin, and Lance's wife Elinor—and the Armstrongs—Simon's benevolent counterpart Daniel Armstrong, his son Kinloch, and Kinloch's wife Ruth. The two families complement each other in a near mirror-image opposition. Simon Gerrard and Daniel Armstrong are ancient enemies whose acrimony has been slowly buried beneath a veneer of affability. Both Lance Gerrard and Kinloch Armstrong stand as heirs apparent to family holdings. Both Kinloch and Lance are in the throes of a difficult marriage to an outsider. Kinloch's mother is dead, and Lance's is so comically ineffectual that her family treats her as if she does not exist. The single Gerrard without an Armstrong counterpart is the insolent, hedonistic Justin, who has inherited all her father's willfulness.

Justin's close encounter with Kinloch Armstrong precedes Spencer's most detailed description of the Gerrards. When she was seventeen, Justin, frustrated by Kinloch's lack of interest in her, had tried to seduce him. Angered by his own desire as well as her haughtiness, Kinloch "pulled her to him and kissed her almost insultingly because he was angry already at himself . . . and at Justin for letting him know that any way you looked at it she was going to win" (77). He finds "a definite revulsion . . . [in] the subtle mixture of give and resistance her flesh offered" and pushes her away. Even Justin's sexual allure cannot overcome his innate distaste for her Gerrard flesh. Spencer writes that "about the Gerrards there was a thickness that had nothing to do with measurement, as marked in Lance's tall frame as in heavy Simon. It seemed that flesh, vein, muscle and bone, instead of finding a separate life and play within the larger, living body, each defining the other, were in them all matted and solidified together, affecting an imperceptible shortening or concealment of joint and tendon, a layered depth of skin" (78). The physical imagery suggests an immoral bloatedness: flesh "matted and solidified," limbs shortened or concealed, and "a layered depth" of deceit and greed.

This unholy genetic bond that unites the Gerrards appears again near the end of the novel when Kinloch accuses Simon of perjury: "Then with a curious deliberation . . . [Simon's] gaze caught up Justin and Lance and seemed to draw them physically near to him in a bond of flesh and blood which was not love, affection or loyalty as the two who watched thought of those things, but which was a quality both shared and potent, though no one on earth, not they

themselves, could have named it." (247). The Gerrards are geneti-
cally linked by greed and arrogance.

Their social prominence is less than a generation old, and their
greed is legendary. When Randall Gibson, a local lawyer, catalogs
the Gerrards for Justin, he is able to reduce them to comic stick
figures of desire: "You all's hearts' desires are simple one word things
and they're written all over every one of you in letters a foot high.
Yes, with Mary Helen, it was marriage and money. With Lance it's
liquor and leisure. See, how they alliterate nicely. You don't do as
well. Men and glamour. L'amour and gla-mour. At least they will
rhyme" (80). Although transparent in their desires, the Gerrards,
particularly Simon and Justin, remain dangerous in their utter contempt for their neighbors.

The title of the novel, *Fire in the Morning*, is also an indirect
reference to the Gerrards. It comes from a Tarsus story about the
burning of a local home by Yankee marauders during the Civil War.
The house was burned in midmorning at the whimsical command
of the Yankee commander, leaving homeless the family that had just
fed him and his men. For Randall Gibson and Kinloch Armstrong,
the careless scorn of the Yankee commander was typified by the
image of a house burning, because of the morning light, in an invisible fire. This invisible flame, they decide separately, is also the closest
analogy they know to the invidious and scornful destruction wrought
by the Gerrards.

If the Gerrards are transparently normal, the Armstrongs are
harder to summarize. Dan Armstrong is sheriff at the time of the
Gerrards' original swindle and must exert all his influence over Tarsus
to prevent the lynching of an innocent black family caught up in the
violence between two white factions. His friend and partner, Felix
McKie, has killed Simon's brother Wills for the cold-blooded murder of a faithful Walston retainer and is blinded in turn by the chance
gunfire of a frightened bystander. Armstrong resigns as sheriff, intending to seek his own justice and the return of his and McKie's
property. Then suddenly, he renounces violent retribution and
allows the coward Simon to take over the town. Daniel Armstrong's
renunciation of revenge is the first clue to the Armstrong character.
He chooses a lifelong course that many in Tarsus consider weak and
cowardly, because he values human dignity—that of others as well
as his own—over possessions and power. His son Kinloch inherits
Daniel's thirst for justice and his habit of ready honesty but, when

the novel opens, has learned neither his father's patience nor his understanding of moral complexity. When Kinloch cries out for revenge, accusing his father of letting Simon Gerrard live, Daniel replies: "Son, son. Listen. A McKie can do wrong. A Walston can do wrong. An Armstrong can do wrong" (149). It is an argument that echoes ironically Ruth's involvement in Ben Gardner's death and Kinloch's own intemperate desire for revenge. Strict justice, Dan Armstrong's life seems to argue, is not enough. It must be tempered by mercy, by the realization of one's own complex culpability.

One of the subtlest aspects of Spencer's portrayal of the two families is the mutual animosity of the younger generation. Long before he knew about the infamous insanity trial of his father's generation, Kinloch Armstrong distrusted and disliked Lance Gerrard. When his new wife, Ruth, asks him to go with her to a party at the Gerrards, it leads to this exchange:

"I don't like to go there," he told her, as he had told her before, except that he spoke almost roughly. "I don't like your going there. No good can come of dealing with the Gerrards. It's best to stay away."
. . . "But why, Kinloch?"
"I don't have any reason," he said. (7)

No reason, Spencer seems to say, other than his moral intuition. Ruth, as a compromise, goes on to the party without him, only to become involved in a fatal prank. In her absence, Kinloch himself wonders about the Gerrards' effect on him, and in a flashback within a flashback, recalls almost telling Ruth about an episode from his childhood. Lance and a gang of boys had tricked Kinloch into playing a game with Kinloch's puppy that led inevitably to the puppy's drowning. Spencer paces the episode with chilling irony; the reader realizes what is happening long before Kinloch, who is desperate to be accepted by the group. Kinloch's humiliation and horror precipitate a series of fistfights with Lance Gerrard, which Kinloch eventually wins. But in winning, he is sucked into a vortex of violence: "Life before had been a steady plane of wandering, hunting, fishing, working around the house. Now he had entered new ground, strange at first, but it took its own place, as the needle of the compass quivers at the point before it rests still and true. He felt some new tie with his father, undefined, but vivid" (26). While he does not feel that a childhood quarrel would justify to Ruth his adult mistrust of Lance and the others, the deeply rooted animosity remains. With it remains an unfortunate self-righteousness, an unreasoning hatred of *all* things Gerrard.[5]

Spencer uses the other significant family groups in the novel more as commentaries than as fully realized portraits. The Guptons of Dark Corners, dangerously violent while at the same time grotesquely funny, serve as reminders to Kinloch Armstrong of his own common humanity. When he saw Mr. Gupton's daughter-in-law for the first time, "he started up from his chair with a cry." He must then apologize.

> "Excuse me, ma'am," said Kinloch. "You looked so much like my wife I thought for a minute it was her."
>
> "Well, she ain't yore wife," said one of the tall men, who sat between them. "She's my wife."
>
> ... With the lowering of the [lamp] chimney, the light climbed to her face and he was again startled to see the leaf-like brown eyes, the clear skin and dark hair, and in addition to feel again the manner that had struck out at him across the breadth of the room, a quality of perpetual evasion along the very path of desire. (209–10)

Kinlock has discovered his own wife's double married to a Gupton, and, implicitly, must see himself as a member of the same extended family of man. Doctor Derryberry, whom Kinloch seeks out because of his testimony at the insanity trial, also reflects on the curious dynamics of family love. Dr. Derryberry tried to avoid being caught up in his own family even after the death of his mother. Describing how he had been left his young niece to tend, he admits to Kinloch, "I had wished to live alone and with this event I began to be afraid" (221). He feared the emotional entrapment and personal sacrifice that all families demand, and ironically what he most feared came to pass when Wills Gerrard forced him to perjure himself for the sake of his niece. Another interesting household in Tarsus consists of Randall Gibson and Cherry Bell, the "fallen" woman of no blood

---

5. Peggy Prenshaw's focus on Kinloch's role as protagonist leads her to conclude that "in the final pages of the novel two central themes merge. The world, embodied in Kinloch's plight, and the burden of history that unfailingly impinges on the individual's effort to be independent and honorable . . . come together." Prenshaw, *Elizabeth Spencer*, 18. This reading is certainly true so far as it goes and highlights the similarities between Spencer's novel and Warren's *All the King's Men*. However, it does not account for the novel's central focus on community or the long passages in which Kinloch plays little or no part.

relation whom his family had taken in years before. A physically and emotionally broken alcoholic, Cherry Bell survives only by the continued care of Randall, who after her death realizes that "for all his harangue to Kinloch, she had been the only thing in Tarsus that was peculiarly his own" (196). She had become, without his knowing it, a vital part of his identity, one of his few ties to Tarsus.

The marriages in *Fire in the Morning* are so significant because for Spencer they represent the forced union of two disparate backgrounds and personalities. The marriages represent the common ground on which two families meet, often in some conflict. They also force the creation of a new communal unit; the intimacy of a successful marriage redefines both parties in their mutual context. Struck by Cherry Bell's death and the unexpected sense of loss it had brought him, Randall Gibson mutters to himself " 'in sickness and health, for better or worse, till death do us part' . . . and forthwith made arrangements for his departure" from Tarsus (196). He realizes that for all his refusal to be categorized by the townspeople, it had been his quite genuine devotion to Cherry Bell that had formed his image in their eyes. Intimate relationships, particularly the long-term intimacy of marriage, fundamentally alter those involved.

Successful marriage in the world of *Fire in the Morning* requires some willingness and ability to adapt, to redirect attention and devotion. Lance and Elinor Gerrard have been married for six years when the novel opens, and though Lance is too self-concerned to notice, Elinor realizes their marriage is little more than a sham. During the detailed dramatic portrait of the Gerrards from the second part of the novel, Elinor reflects ruefully to herself that

you can't get a divorce because your father-in-law's got so much money your husband doesn't have to work. You can't claim incompatibility when your husband doesn't believe any of the things you've never believed either, and if you've always had a honing towards those things you've never believed, it's not his fault he hasn't got the honing too. (You get the honing from your folks, I guess, and it's for the things they really do believe in, though you'd never say you believed in them, too; and Lance's folks haven't got any idea what I'm talking about.) And I can't charge mental cruelty, because it's my own mind that's doing it to me. I could charge infidelity, of course, because I'm as sure of that as I'm sure of the difference between black and white, but there's never been anything flagrant or extended, and besides I've got enough pride not to want to throw it all away before a courtroom. (188)

Ironically, she is quite close to the emotional and psychological truth of her outrage at Lance and his family without realizing it: When she describes the "honing" she feels for the Christian virtues of her parents, she is expressing her own desire to believe. Although she, like Randall Gibson, plays the carefree cynic, she is at heart as moral a being as Ruth or Kinloch Armstrong. She is as instinctively repulsed by her sister-in-law Justin as is Kinloch Armstrong, at one point barely stopping herself from slapping Justin in midconversation. She constantly chips away at the Gerrards' selfishness and superiority. Instead of a honing for honesty and affection, Lance has inherited the Gerrards' monolithic egotism, an instinct to reject all that is not blood kin. When challenged by Kinloch at the end of the novel, Simon Gerrard counters by having Justin write out a formal accusation of Ruth's complicity in Ben Gardner's death. "You'll never get my name on that thing," Elinor tells him. "It doesn't concern you . . . as Lance well knows," Simon answers (247). Elinor leaves Lance that very day, not because of his shabby immorality—she has known about that for years—but because she could no longer ignore his unwillingness to deny his father's influence. She knew finally that Lance, like the vicious Justin, stemmed "from old Simon" (184) and that his attachment to his father prevented any fundamental intimacy with her.

The confrontation between the Gerrards and Kinloch Armstrong also precipitates a crisis in Kinloch's marriage to Ruth. When Simon has Justin testify to Ruth's guilt, Kinloch is shocked into silence. However, "it did not occur to him to think of her as separate from himself; to him the death of Ben Gardner was something he himself had done and simply lost from his mind. It belonged to him, at least, and if the burden of it landed on his back at the wrong time, that was his hard luck. Yet think of her he did, as though she were an unexplained part of his nature that he did not understand and could not control" (246).

Under the effect of this strange and sudden shock, Kinloch realizes for the first time his oneness with Ruth. He had fallen in love with her originally because "she [was] . . . so strange to things . . . and different from them all"(5). Their early relationship, though full of wonder and gentle discovery, is a litany of small mysteries and misunderstandings. As he tried to explain his antipathy for the Gerrards, "she sat idly turning a gold bracelet on her wrist. It had belonged to his mother and he had given it to her. She did not speak for a while, and as often happened, he had no earthly idea what she was thinking" (37). After Ben Gardner's death, Ruth is obsessed with the need to tell Kinloch, to trust him completely, as he asks, but she cannot predict how he will react and so fears him. Her fear sends her scurrying away to New York. There, Randall Gibson asks her, "Who in the name of God struck you both tongue-tied?" (234), and she is at a loss to explain.

Spencer makes it clear that what had struck them "both tongue-tied" was their disparate backgrounds, their mutual inability to intuit the other's feelings. However, while talking to Randall, she realizes suddenly the full measure of her devotion to Kinloch, who hundreds of miles away is reaching the same conclusion in Simon Gerrard's office. From that moment, they are speeding—she literally, he figuratively—toward each other. Their stuttering, stumbling, but honest reunion leaves Ruth fully a member of the Armstrong family and Kinloch with a new awareness of himself as a dedicated husband and less-than-perfect man. Spencer uses their relationship to dramatize how crisis can meld two dissimilar but devoted people together. The emotional trauma of doubt and separation becomes the shared history that they had, to this point, lacked.

The rebirth of their marriage, coupled with the death of his father, enables Kinloch to resolve his own ambiguity toward the larger world of Tarsus itself. The action of the entire novel, past as well as present, occurs within the brooding communal watchfulness of the town. Much has been written about the agrarian nature of the South, how the region remained a land of farming and identification with the soil through recent generations. A setting that is just as significant and yet has had less scholarly attention is the small southern town. Small towns in the Deep South remained fundamentally isolated, self-contained units well into the twentieth century. To the degree that the citizens were socially conscious, they were conscious of their status in the town, with little or no regard for the world beyond. Tarsus, Mississippi, remains a shadowy but ever present force in *Fire in the Morning*, and Spencer's portrait of Tarsus pays detailed attention to the ways various characters react to life there.[6]

Randall Gibson is in many ways the communal voice of Tarsus.

---

6. Spencer has noted more than once that she modeled both Tarsus and Lacey, Mississippi, the setting of *The Voice at the Back Door*, on her hometown of Carrollton.

Part oral historian, part barometer of public opinion, part artistic observer, and totally obsessed with Tarsus, he dominates the second section of the novel. Spencer has remarked in several interviews on the type of educated southerner, often a lawyer, for whom the town's history becomes avocation as well as vocation. "The Southern lawyer," she once said, "is a character in everybody's work on the South. The lawyer is most always the university trained individual on the scene and so became the traditional spokesman of a community. The law was the profession for the gentry to go into because it often wasn't a profession at all. . . . I'm not sure that this character has ever been fully treated in Southern literature. . . . That type of intellectual Southerner really existed and has never been fully realized."[7]

Randall Gibson views himself as the one human unknown in the town's complex equation. He tells Justin Gerrard: "Talking about me is something I do not object to; I simply deplore it as a waste of breath. Every time you talk about a person you assume he wants something and that something you think he wants is what you consciously or unconsciously attack. With me you are defeated before you start. I want nothing" (79). He has fended off the town's inquiring gaze by "indirect means and by direct ridicule. After all, nothing Tarsus thought of him could injure him as long as Tarsus could not define him" (61).

And yet even the garrulous, world-weary Randall Gibson underestimates Tarsus' influence in his life. After Cherry Bell's death, he prepares to abandon the town for the anonymity of New York. When Kinloch asks where he will go, he replies simply, "Where I have no identity" (196). He is the prototype for the many characters in Spencer's fiction who abandon a ready-made life because of the pressures of communal awareness. He flees Tarsus when he is forced to realize just how much a part of the web of identity he had become. "For all I have denounced Tarsus," he admits to Kinloch, "I am inescapably a part of it, and sometimes when I am very drunk, I come half-way to love it" (107). In abandoning his love-hate affair with the town, he is abandoning a life in which everyone he meets on the street knows him intimately.

Prior to his departure, Spencer uses Gibson to study the artistic

7. Roberts, "Whole Personality," in *Conversations with Elizabeth Spencer*, ed. Prenshaw, 233–34.

sensibility trapped in small-town community life. As he tells Kinloch, he is a "stranger who was born among them" (103). He knows their ways as well as any one person can and yet studies them from an emotional distance. The objectivity he has constructed out of his education, his reading, and his self-conscious cynicism makes him an expert observer. He translates his observations into highly entertaining narrative; in the second section of the novel, he telescopes the entire history of the Gerrards in Tarsus into thirty-five pages of description and dialogue. He opens with the disclaimer "I cannot understand it. I simply give the facts" (108). But he immediately begins to embroider, analyze, and create. He describes blind Felix McKie's "eyes—hard, bright, intense blue eyes that we never saw" (122)—and countless other details that he could only have imagined.[8] His is the story within the story of *Fire in the Morning*, and his telling of it triggers Kinloch Armstrong's desire for revenge.

Appropriately, Kinloch plans that revenge within the context of Tarsus public opinion. Prior to this time, Tarsus had accepted the Gerrards in their midst with an eerie, unaccountable approval. Even Randall Gibson is mystified.

What shall we say when people come along whose violence and greed is open, who place no value at all on the respectable thing except as it serves their definite and always visible ends? . . . Should the Gerrards live in Tarsus a thousand years, the record of every friendly gesture will show the purpose as their own gain, while their every idle minute will be filled with laughter at our expense, contempt for us, or more often, simple disregard. And these are the people we have allowed to all but own us, all but rule us. Never a hand called. I cannot understand it. (108)

The Gerrards, Simon and his brother Wills, had manipulated the town's distrust of Kinloch Walston in order to have him declared insane. So it is appropriate that when Kinloch finally confronts Simon years later, he demands not legal retribution but communal justice: "I don't know as I'm easy enough with the law to think there aren't ways to get justice quicker and surer. I offer you the chance to publish a statement saying that Kinloch Walston was never insane and that all your property was therefore obtained on a false basis. You need not be afraid because I will not pursue the case if you will

---

8. Although the book's other characters as well as its critics generally ignore the issue, Spencer subtly questions Randall Gibson's reliability and the relativity of narrative "truth" in general.

then proceed to offer your land at auction, *all of it*, so that not one acre of what was once Walston can ever be Gerrard again. That's what I want" (243).

He renounces the land, which except for the Gerrards he would have inherited. Instead he wants some finer sense of communal wholeness to be returned. "Me and a lot of other people live in Tarsus," he explains to Elinor, and "I for one have felt every day I can remember that something was wrong here and that I couldn't live here right until it was gone" (243). Even Simon Gerrard is shaken by the power of this threat. He demands of Lance, who is reluctant to sign Justin's countercharge: "You set on playing the fool? You want to see me and your mother and sister talked about, your family turned into a laughing stock before this whole town?" (247). Although the confrontation goes unresolved when Kinloch refuses Simon's offer of mutual secrecy, this meeting sparks sudden and drastic change in individual lives. Kinloch and Ruth reunite, and Elinor leaves Lance, both of whom give up Tarsus as a home.

Kinloch and Ruth's decision to stay on in Tarsus after Daniel Armstrong's death is indicative of a significant pattern in the novel. Except for Felix McKie, they are the only two central characters who remain in Tarsus at the end of the book. The old antagonists, Daniel Armstrong and Simon Gerrard, are dead. Randall Gibson has already left, fleeing "identity." Elinor Dudley Gerrard has found the impetus to leave Lance and return to her family. After his father's death, even Lance Gerrard feels compelled to auction off the Gerrard estate and leave the town where he had for years played the role of prince of the ruling family. "I can't stand the sight of this town any longer," he tells Kinloch (274). Predictably, "Justin was preparing to leave and seek her fortune in New York" (270). The original community has dissolved under the residual pressure of the feud and the influence of the outsiders, Elinor and Ruth. As the novel closes, Spencer deftly suggests that the question of whether to go or stay is the first question any southerner must ask. It is the southerner's primary existential issue, and once it is decided, then life can take its form.

Kinloch and Ruth Armstrong live on in Tarsus; they raise together the money Ruth is fined after she admits her involvement in Gardner's death. They settle peacefully because they finally, after suffering the throes of a difficult labor, bear a true communion, a genuine marriage of spirit and body. In the closing scene, Spencer reveals indirectly that Ruth is joyously pregnant. Their successful reunion has freed both to solve the larger issues of Gardner's death and the Gerrards' treachery; together they naturally accomplish what neither could manage alone. In this way, Spencer weaves her various communities together—private decisions mysteriously solving public dilemmas and public actions changing the course of private intimacies.

It is obvious from early in the novel that individual characters cannot be separated from the context of their marriages, their families, and the community at large. The subtler message becomes clear at the end: The community itself exists only in the context of the individual perception of it. Tarsus, Mississippi, is a psychological as well as geographical reality. In emphasizing this point, Spencer exhibits some signs of what would become her characteristic narrative experimentation. As Prenshaw first noted, the "structural shifts in voice and time, which link the numerous consciousnesses in the novel, embody the theme of interrelatedness, suggesting the close connection between hero and community."[9] More specifically, Spencer uses a roving limited omniscience to center the reader's point of view in first one character and then another. There are also long sections narrated by Elinor Gerrard and Randall Gibson. Although these techniques are certainly not original, Spencer does use them for an original purpose—to weave a communal point of view that emphasizes no one character.

What is finally most significant about *Fire in the Morning* is not that it stakes out yet another fictional territory in Mississippi but rather that it defines the emotional and psychological territory that Elizabeth Spencer will eventually master. In this and succeeding novels, she portrays the complex reality of dynamic, interlocking communities—the social milieu that, internalized, forms the individual. Herbert Creekmore's original judgment that the value of this novel lay in its insightful portrait of "a complex of people" has since proved prophetic, as Spencer has gone on to discover more sophisticated narrative means to her artistic ends—the study of people bound in layers of relationships.

9. Prenshaw, *Elizabeth Spencer*, 27.

2 / *This Crooked Narrative Way*

I think religion is dangerous. I really do. I think it can almost poison human relations.

—Elizabeth Spencer, in an interview

In the past ten years, Spencer's reputation has begun to climb back toward the status it enjoyed in the late 1950s and early 1960s, just after the publication of the critically successful and popular books *The Voice at the Back Door* (1956) and *The Light in the Piazza* (1960). Partly because of the success of her collection *The Short Stories of Elizabeth Spencer* (1981), it is only now that Spencer's more sophisticated but lesser known novels—*This Crooked Way* (1952), *No Place for an Angel* (1967), and *The Snare* (1972)—are beginning to receive the scholarly attention they deserve. These three novels are alike in that they are all ambitiously experimental books that in some way or other failed to match critics' preconceptions of her work and eventually passed out of print, leaving her reputation to fade until recently.

This Crooked Way is also particularly interesting because in it Spencer attempted for the first time a narrative structure to complement her thematic concerns. The novel centers upon the life of an ambitious Mississippi planter named Amos Dudley. Dudley is a religious fanatic, though not in a public, proselytizing way. Rather he seeks from adolescence to prove through the pattern and visions of his life that he has been especially blessed by God. His self-obsession alienates him from family, lovers, friends, and even his wife—leaving in him a moral crookedness that he does not recognize until the end of the novel. Spencer narrates Dudley's story in a "crooked" fashion that captures the dangers of his obsession both to himself and to others. She has called it her "most original book"; it is a daring and, in some ways, difficult novel.[1]

In narrative structure and plot, *This Crooked Way* is similar to two major Faulkner novels. Its multiple narrators bring to mind *The Sound and the Fury*, and Amos Dudley's rise to power recalls that of Thomas Sutpen in *Absalom, Absalom!* Although Spencer denies any conscious reference to Faulkner, his novels form an instructive context. In *Absalom, Absalom!* Faulkner creates a hero who is tragically larger than life, a man, Thomas Sutpen, who is transformed into myth before the reader's eyes. Spencer reverses the process with Amos Dudley; he is reduced in the last section of *This Crooked Way* from myth to mere humanity and so saved from destruction. Spencer manages this transformation through reversing another Faulknerian pattern, the narrative progression of *The Sound and the Fury*. Whereas Faulkner resolves a series of fragmented first-person narratives with the omniscient final section centered on Dilsey, Spencer resolves her fragmented tale by shifting the point of view to *inside* the main character. In doing so, she reveals to the reader that Amos Dudley is a member of the human community that he had for so many years spurned.

Amos Dudley is saved by God from drowning when he is sixteen years old. "God had," Amos considered, "snatched a knot in him" in order to warn him, both of the dangers of impudence and the power of prayer.[2] From that moment, Amos feels himself "a child of God," marked for special achievement. He parlays this simple faith and years of backbreaking labor into a thriving plantation and an affluent marriage.[3] To those who would emphasize his similarity

1. Elizabeth Pell Broadwell and Ronald Wesley Hoag, "A Conversation with Elizabeth Spencer," in *Conversations with Elizabeth Spencer,* ed. Prenshaw, 64.

2. Elizabeth Spencer, *This Crooked Way* (New York, 1952), 13. Hereinafter cited by page number in the text. As Prenshaw notes, there are "some striking parallels . . . in the portrayals of Amos's vision" and the self-baptism/self-destruction of the child Harry in Flannery O'Connor's "The River," first published in 1953, a year after *This Crooked Way*. Prenshaw, *Elizabeth Spencer,* 34.

3. Amos Dudley's similarities to the Old Testament's Jacob are even more marked than those of Kinloch Armstrong to Saul of Tarsus in *Fire in the Morning*. In the Broadwell and Hoag interview (1980), Spencer admits, "There's a literal parallel between the two men." She notes that "in the Bible, Jacob operates like a businessman with God, making bargains and trading things off. Amos, too, tries to deal in this fashion." Broadwell and Hoag, "Conversation," in *Conversations with Elizabeth Spencer,* ed. Prenshaw, 63–64.

to Faulkner's Sutpen, Spencer has replied, "Amos Dudley didn't want the trappings of success so much as the literal proof that he was a God-directed man."[4] His forty-five-year search for this proof not only alienates him from his friends, wife, and children, it comes perilously close to destroying all of those around him. The novel is, in fact, a case study of religious fanaticism's ability to deny intimacy and kill community.

This Crooked Way is divided into five parts. In the first, Spencer examines Dudley's adolescence and young manhood from a third-person omniscient perspective, specifically using him as a Jamesian "center of consciousness" through which to view his world. She then, in parts two through four, narrates his rise to prosperity through the first-person voices of his best friend, his niece, and his wife. She titles these three middle sections of the novel "indictments," and in them Amos is accused in turn by "the three people . . . who had the most to make him answer for."[5] At the end of the third indictment the narrator, Amos' wife Ary, murders the man Amos intended to marry to their daughter. This is the most suspenseful moment in the book, as neither narrator nor reader can predict what Amos' reaction will be.

Nor can the reader predict the point of view from which it will be related. In a long, poetic final section, Spencer portrays Amos Dudley's recovery through his own personality and voice. It is an abrupt shock, bringing as it does a shift in setting, tone, and diction as well as narrative stance. This is multiple narration with a vengeance, a gamble in technique that in the eyes of several reviewers did not pay off. R. W. Flint found "the whole final third person narrative [*sic*] . . . hurried and stuffed with adventurous excitements so that the end of this novel is decidedly a clutter." Flint goes on to generalize, based on *This Crooked Way,* that "the ability to manage endings may be on the decline." Writing more than thirty years later, Peggy Prenshaw devotes an entire section of her discussion of the novel to "the problem of the ending." Spencer herself emphasizes that early readers had what Prenshaw understated as "strongly mixed reactions"

4. Terry Roberts, unpublished interview with Elizabeth Spencer, September 10, 1990.

5. Roberts, "Whole Personality," in *Conversations with Elizabeth Spencer,* ed. Prenshaw, 225.

to the ending.[6] Despite this initial response, it is clear that the last section provides a rounding out of the novel in tone as well as plot. It establishes Amos' humanity for the reader just as he is returning to the human community of his wife and family, and it does so through a daring shift in point of view. Time and distance have clarified what contemporary critics failed to see—the link between Spencer's theme and her decision to end the novel as she did.

Unwound from its crooked telling, the story of Amos Dudley is a fairly simple one. After his self-baptism and miraculous escape from drowning at sixteen, he grows more and more ambitious, seeking a wider scope for financial gain. His ambition brings him into direct conflict with his family, and he eventually leaves Yacona, his birthplace, for the Delta with his best friend, Arney Talliafero. Amos takes advantage of the frontier atmosphere of the Delta, eventually trading himself into possession of six hundred acres of "matted wilderness" (50), which he intends to transform, as proof of God's blessing, into a thriving plantation.

Dudley's personal relations after this point are poisoned by his ambition, however, and it takes a dramatic murder in his own home forty-five years later to break the hold his vision has on him. Spencer dramatizes his decline with a series of narratives "as crooked as [his] life."[7] After the opening section, a third-person exposition of Dudley's childhood, she portrays him from three separate angles through the series of "indictments," which suggest just how deluded he has become. In the last section of the novel, he finally speaks "for himself" as the shock of his wife's murder of their prospective son-in-law forces him back into the reality of human community.

The opening section of the novel is entitled quite pointedly "The Wandering," a reference to the Old Testament wanderings of Jacob in particular as well as to those of any individual or group seeking God's direction. Dudley's years of wandering in the Delta begin with his experiencing a miracle on his way home from the annual Tabernacle, a huge country revival meeting. After hearing a sermon on Jacob and blessedness, he takes a short cut home, intending to

6. R. W. Flint, "Recent Fiction," *Hudson Review*, I (1949), 590; Prenshaw, *Elizabeth Spencer*, 42–45.
7. Roberts, "Whole Personality," in *Conversations with Elizabeth Spencer*, ed. Prenshaw, 225.

ford the Yacona River. He is swept away by the current and nearly drowned. Realizing that he had subconsciously set out to baptize himself, he cries out against God in fear. Then comes what for the rest of his life he would believe a miracle.

Whatever came to him came from behind, unseen by him forever, a hand stretched down from behind to lift him up. He felt the strike and pull of fiery pain in his right shoulder, the lightening and life of his whole body. He saw, as he passed upward, the high bank fleeing by. . . . Then mud, bank, and water dropped far beneath him, like stars falling under the earth instead of over it, and there was only the fire in his shoulder and the easy sweep of the round earth.

He could not remember coming back down again. His next consciousness was of sitting calm as mid-afternoon at the top of the bank with his feet dangling off the edge toward the water and his hands crossed idly in his lap. His clothes were dry and there was no mud on him anywhere. (12)

The physical wound left by God's touch is reminiscent of Jacob's biblical wrestling match with God that Spencer here alludes to. Genesis 32:24–30 describes what happens after another wanderer has sent his retinue on across the river "over the ford Jabbok."

And Jacob was left alone; and there wrestled a man with him until the breaking of the day.

And when he saw that he prevailed not against him, he touched the hollow of his thigh; and the hollow of Jacob's thigh was out of joint, as he wrestled with him.

And he said, Let me go, for the day breaketh. And he said, I will not let thee go, except thou bless me.

And he said unto him, What is thy name? And he said, Jacob.

And he said, Thy name shall be called no more Jacob, but Israel: for as a prince hast thou power with God and with men, and hast prevailed.

And Jacob asked him, and said, Tell me, I pray thee, thy name. And he said, Wherefore is it that thou dost ask after my name? And he blessed him there.

And Jacob called the name of the place Peniel: for I have seen God face to face, and my life is preserved.

Amos, like Jacob after his fording of the river, feels himself to be "a child of God" and begins to form in his imagination the articles of a contract that will prove such to be the case. Those articles—wealth, affluent marriage, offspring—are also distinctly Old Testament in flavor. The whole episode, in fact, reflects the biblical obsessions of Christian fundamentalists across the South. However, unlike another student of southern religious fervor, Flannery O'Connor, Spencer is primarily concerned with the impact her protagonist's miracle has on his life in this world rather than the next.

Spencer has remarked bluntly that fundamentalism "poisons . . . personal relations."[8] In Amos Dudley's case, his self-obsessed fascination with his contract, his "design" as he calls it, divorces him from any mere human intimacy. He begins at the moment of his miracle to lead an emotionally crippled life, made crooked by his alienation from others. Significantly, the evangelist's voice at Tabernacle "was the first and last voice he ever paid close attention to in his life" (7). But after the sermon, he "did not want to see the preacher close. It was no human hand he wished to touch when he took the dark way home alone" (9). He intends never to be baptized by a "human hand"; rather, he thinks, "I will do it myself and for myself, and that way it will be right" (10). From the moment of his self-baptism, he is a wanderer in the Old Testament sense. Years later, when he is on the brink of success, he returns to Yacona for his father's funeral and is shocked to realize that the whole town mourns: "All of them, thought Amos. He was so quiet, and all of them his friends" (73). He is stunned because, with the exception of Arney Talliafero and Thelma Dubard, he has allowed himself no friendly human contact. Eventually even these two will abandon him when they realize that for Amos no other human being is fundamentally real.

Amos' self-isolation eventually frightens all who know him well. The first "indictment" of his selfishness (the novel's second section) comes from Arney Talliafero, the friend who joined him in building his Delta plantation. When Arney first arrives at Cypress Landing, he and Amos settle into a comfortable household with Thelma Dubard. After Thelma rejects—with a cast-iron skillet—Arney's secret advances, the three fall into an easy, natural rhythm.

We latched up together nice enough. Amos bossing the place. . . . And Thelma for him— . . . I thought Amos might go on ahead and marry her sometime. And me—well, nothing really for me except liking to be there with them since Thelma taken the skillet and aimed to keep on taking it, and I was handy to be called on and the fishing was good. Everything set together in a sort of circle in my head: the place and Amos, Amos and Thelma, Thelma and the skillet, me and Amos, me and fishing and whatever

8. *Ibid.*

else. A circle is a good way to live because you can keep on going around it and don't never wind up nowheres else. (91)

Arney realizes that outside forces threaten their emotional equilibrium. He first sees that something "didn't set right" when Amos returns from his father's funeral "lowrat[ing] his folks" (91). Amos had returned claiming his family "all wished ill" to him, trying to trap him into remaining in Yacona and giving up the plantation (77). Arney knows Amos well enough to sense in his paranoia the seeds of alienation from all family intimacy. Then when Ary Morgan visits Cypress Landing for the first time, Arney knows the circle is in danger: "Don't ask me how I know Ary Morgan was connected up with [Amos' rejection of his family]. She just was, that's all I know. One thing like that you forget about, two and you're unsettled" (91). Thelma tries to hold Amos solely with her sexual allure and, in so doing, becomes pregnant. Even that is not enough to hold Amos, however, and during Arney's last night at Cypress Landing, he realizes that "somebody had done stamped out the circle we had been treading around. I didn't know who had done it, but I knowed it was gone" (95). Arney soon realizes that it is Amos' desire for Ary Morgan that has destroyed their rhythm. Both Thelma and Arney leave Cypress Landing that night, abandoning Amos to his scheme. What both never see, however, is that Amos has broken up their home for Ary Morgan not because of her attraction as a woman but because of her attraction as a symbol.

The Amos Dudley that we see through Arney Talliafero's indictment is a pitiful, scheming man. He has fallen so low in servitude to his plan that by the time Arney walks out on him, he cannot abide the sight of Amos. The transition, then, from this despicable figure to the frighteningly powerful Amos Dudley of the next section requires an imaginative leap on the part of the reader. Whereas Arney Talliafero's Amos had been a friendly, country-bred man done in by ambition, the Amos of the third section is a calculatingly cold figure who looms larger than life. In altering her readers' perception of the character both here and later in the novel, Spencer succeeds again and again in frustrating their desire to define him; as each character in turn fails to penetrate, to know, Amos Dudley, his mystery mounts for readers as well.

Dolly, the narrator of the third section, is the daughter of Ary's sister Louise, the fabled Delta debutante against whose beauty and charm both Ary and Dolly have been measured all their lives. After her mother's death when she is four years old, Dolly is passed from relative to relative. She settles on her Uncle Amos' as her favorite place because there she is neither pitied nor spoiled: "His house . . . was a heart of happiness" (103). Dolly, however, like Arney Talliafero before her, begins to sense a rift in the Dudley household. Because she lives on the boundary between Amos on one hand and the Morgan family on the other, she is sensitive from early childhood to the distrust and dislike each party feels for the other. As she grows older, she becomes increasingly aware that her Morgan cousins have graduated to frilly dresses and finishing schools while she still roams the farm in torn jeans. Her allegiance remains with Amos, however, until she realizes that he does not return her love. When the Morgans threaten to send Dolly to their chosen finishing school, Amos rips their application letter in half, "convicted in every eye [except Dolly's] of unforgivable rudeness" (115). She is thrilled until she later overhears Amos admit to the distraught Ary that he had done it only for himself.

"You cannot say you did it because you love her," [Ary] said. . . . "There is no other reason to take and tear and trample down except love . . . but you did not do it for love?"

"That's right," he said easily. . . . "I did it for myself." (115–16)

The fourteen-year-old Dolly suddenly realizes that Ary fears Amos, and she in turn inherits the fear that comes from alienation: "For all things that had seemed one now stood separate: trees from water, barns from house, cabins from field, Negroes from master, 'Tary from Uncle Amos, I from all else. In separation many become weak, and many become meaningless. I was both" (116).

Like Arney's circle, Dolly's dream of "a heart of happiness" compounded of the people she loved has been "stamped out." She, like Arney, faces up to Amos but is even more honest, more insightful. Knowing that "his pride had shut him from" her, she admits to him that she must return to the Morgans because she fears him (118). The lonely, pitiable Amos Dudley abandoned by Arney Talliafero has become, in Dolly's eyes, "lonely and bright and powerful, like the sun" (116). Although he is as lonely and distant as ever, his need for others seems to shrink as his power and vision grow.

It would seem from Dolly's testimony that no human being could possibly penetrate Amos' secret obsession with God, but Ary Morgan Dudley's indictment of her husband in part four reveals "an accuser who matches Amos in strength of character."[9] In the reflection of her will, his own shrinks to at least human proportions. After they have lost their first two children as well as another possible son to miscarriage, the conflict between Amos and Ary comes to a head over their last child. Following Ary's miscarriage, which Amos accuses her of inducing, he changes the name of their daughter Mary Louise to Dinah Lee Dudley, seeking to erase any Morgan tendencies in her. Under her father's influence, Dinah begins to resemble subtly the son he desired—wearing worn-out jeans and men's shirts.

But Amos' design goes beyond the complete possession of Dinah. He grooms for her the young drifter Joe Ferguson, a man Amos senses is so like himself that he will through marriage claim Ferguson as a son. Ary's revelation that Ferguson has used Amos' influence to seduce Dinah while simultaneously carrying on a bestial affair with an albino woman does not even faze Amos. He also remains calm before her further charge that Ferguson may well be Amos' son by Thelma Dubard and that Amos has suspected it all along. He is so obsessed by the completion of his God-oriented design that even the incestuous violation of his daughter seems inconsequential. It seems so because he believes that if Ferguson is his son, then he can somehow legitimatize him with the marriage, thereby exorcising his guilt over Thelma Dubard. Again, his motives are stunningly self-centered.

In a sense, Joe Ferguson *is* Amos and Ary's child, for he is like both in disturbing ways, and his status at Dudley is the product of their disharmony. Amos' protégé Ferguson has a strangely intimate, symbiotic relationship with Ary. "You're different," he tells her at one point. "Different from them. You're more like me" (169–70). She is shocked not only at his effrontery but also at the truth of what he says. As much as she instinctively dislikes and distrusts Ferguson, she senses they are the two outsiders inside the Dudley household. Later she admits to herself: "It was pleasant for me to be in his company. It seemed that we were, of all on Dudley, the only two who were entirely sane" (191). There is, then, in this odd quadrangle of father, mother, daughter, and disturbingly familiar outsider, a sort of fluid family unit—a unit whose final shape remains a desperate question for both Amos and Ary. At the height of their dispute over

9. Prenshaw, *Elizabeth Spencer*, 40.

Ferguson as a prospective son(-in-law), Amos tells Ary that he must act alone.

> "The road I . . . got shoved on to had to be walked by nobody but me, and them you give the chance to walk with you will cross you up, or kill themselves trying. . . ."
>
> "You are shutting me out," [she] said, "at the very time that matters to me most."
>
> "I can't help that."
>
> He turned away from [her] . . . and stood looking up at the great, blue, empty sky. . . .
>
> Now [she] was afraid. (195–96)

She fears his inscrutability, his unwillingness to be moved by any human agent, including her.

Ary's solution to the Gordian knot her family has become is to act decisively. Once she is sure that nothing she can say will deter Amos from marrying Joe Ferguson to Dinah, she murders Ferguson in the hallway of their house. In doing so, she frees herself of the Morgans, paying, as she describes it, "my debt to them and their debt to the world. . . . I was free of them, and the measure and proof of my freedom was that I was alone. I had forsaken all others; my wedding night had come at last. I would face Amos Dudley alone" (217).

She has, in fact, sliced through the bewildering knot of relationships that had prevented her from a true union with Amos. In murdering Ferguson, Ary destroys that in Amos which she could not understand; she murdered Ferguson to keep from having to destroy her husband. Ironically, without knowing it, she has at the same time destroyed his chance at completing his design and so freed him of his God-directed path. As she sits beside Ferguson's body waiting for Amos, she is no longer "afraid, but [her] heart picked up speed, racing faster and faster, like a bride's heart paced to the setting sun" (218). The novel pauses at this juncture—the end pointedly of Ary's indictment—in a sort of suspended animation that may mark the eve of Amos and Ary Dudley's true marriage, the beginning of their true intimacy. In murdering Joe Ferguson, the offspring of their differences, she has freed each to accept the other.

By this point in the novel Spencer has carefully woven the three indictments together with imagery and diction, creating a sense of continuity and wholeness despite the three quite distinct narrators.

The house Amos plans to build in Arney's indictment is lovingly described by Dolly, only to become the scene of Ferguson's murder in Ary's section. At the end of the second indictment, the frightened, lonely Dolly "lay on the sofa in the empty hall and watched for a ghost" (118). The twentieth word of the next section, Ary's indictment, is *ghost*: "Louise living had a ghost with her. Louise dead left the ghost behind. The ghost was what they thought she was; and though I knew what she really was, I contended with a ghost" (121).

These are only two of many examples of devices Spencer uses to sew the three indictments together. The result is a chorus of voices that tend to harmonize, to blend in such a way that instead of emphasizing the relativity of perspective, they emphasize the community of perspective. The three speakers and the others they describe are worked into a kind of quilt of relationships in which there is one notable gap—Amos Dudley. The three indictments make it obvious that all the other characters in the novel seek to define themselves in terms of one another and of him. Only Amos seeks to define himself as independent of human community, in terms only of his vision of God. What disparity, what fracture, what crookedness there is in the community of Dudley, Mississippi, results from the tear in communal relations caused by Amos' alienation.

The continuity of the three indictments, then, as well as Amos' fierce independence, sets the stage for the shock caused by the dramatic shift in tone of the last section. As Spencer herself has explained, she had foreseen the novel clearly as she wrote it up through Ferguson's murder. However, "I didn't foresee what would happen after the murder, but when I got there in the writing, I felt that the energy was coming from [Amos Dudley]. . . . He at this point had either reached a dead end in his life or he had to take off in a new way. Well, suddenly the writing itself took off in the way *he* wanted it to go." Spencer titles Amos Dudley's "new way" simply "Return"; in his own voice Amos narrates his return from forty-five years of wandering in an emotional desert. As Spencer put it: "I had a choice at the end of the third indictment to make it either a tragedy or to relate it back to the strong, life-giving elements in the story. I obviously chose the latter. . . . Up to that point, [Amos] thought the life force in him was the only thing there was. He had to get outside himself in order to belong." [10]

10. Roberts, "Whole Personality," in *Conversations with Elizabeth Spencer,* ed. Prenshaw, 222, 225.

Ironically, Amos' getting *outside* himself leads the reader, along with the other characters, to get *inside* him. From the beginning of the three indictments, the voices have defined Amos as negative space, which neither the other characters nor the reader could penetrate. In contrast, from the first line he speaks in "Return," Amos Dudley becomes a warm, living sensibility—an ironic, rueful, and eventually even loving man.

Those closest to him have indicted him for shutting them out of the core of his life. He is, as far as they or the reader can tell, a profoundly disconnected man. The shock of Ferguson's murder and, even more, the vision of Ary's face hovering over the corpse strip him of the illusions that had bound him.

I took three steps into the hall when I saw and took in what had happened, but it was not the thing that had happened that stopped me cold.

She sat in the straight chair with her legs crossed and the little gun hanging from one hand and her back growing straight up out of her seat, and above, way, way above, was her face. I saw it like a speck of a bird way up in the empty sky at a clear sunset and I saw it too like a leaf by the porch that the spyglass picks up when I study to see way off if the tractor's broke down. She had gone to some place way away from the gun in her hand, or the body on the floor, or the thing she had done. (223–24)

From that point, he discovers his humanity: He discovers it for Ary by taking the blame for the murder and returning to her waiting circle of homelife; he discovers it for himself by letting go of his secrets and accepting, after forty-five years, the circle of his family; he discovers it for the reader by taking the narrative full circle back to where it had begun.[11] He opens simultaneously for all three an emotional depth, a capacity for humility and humor, forgiveness and acceptance.

In speaking for himself, he becomes for both readers and other characters a part of the human chorus. He explains to a construction worker that he meets that all his life he had been "tangled up with God" (235); in finally untangling himself he releases his own humanity. Significantly, for this is at the heart of Spencer's theme, he finally does so by honoring the humanity of others. All along, he finally admits, he had "had to count on [people] more than [he] knew"

11. Although Amos allows the Morgans to believe he killed Ferguson and even contrives to have his brother-in-law, a minister, help him dispose of the body, the final section is uninterrupted by the local sheriff. If Spencer means the final section to be read as strict realism, this is an obvious, if well-hidden, flaw.

(276). The final section of *This Crooked Way* came as a shock to some reviewers not only because of the shift in narrative perspective; that technique was by 1952 almost a modernist cliché. It was also a shock because the shift in perspective created a profound shift in tone.

What had become increasingly tragic, increasingly suspenseful, is quite suddenly released by Amos' rueful, self-deprecating reflections. As surprised as the reader by Ary's murder of Ferguson, he returns by instinct to Yacona in search of his family. In Yacona, he discovers his entire family about to be flooded out by a federal dam project. Volunteering to be baptized in their presence, he then takes them back with him to Dudley along the road he had followed forty-five years before. In every respect the final section is a radical shift in perspective; it is also a radical return to the landscape, the diction, even the plotting of the opening scenes of the novel. The tone is genuinely comic in several instances: Amos' stunned lack of direction, Ary's utter disregard for Morgan kin, Amos' return to Ary accompanied by a family straight out of Erskine Caldwell. And ultimately, the tone of Amos' voice and the tenor of his reborn personality foster a tremendous release of tension. What at the end of Act IV has all the earmarks of a classical tragedy ends instead as a tragicomedy, a dark tale snatched from the jaws of disaster by the triumph of community over individual pride.[12] As in the classical theater, newfound communal equilibrium is symbolized by marriage—in this case, the final spiritual union of Amos and Ary Morgan. Ironically, what may have thrown early reviewers is the radically new "old way" in which Spencer used her multiple narrators.

Amos Dudley's forty-five-year obsession with the signs and symbols of grace cuts him off from what might have truly helped him identify himself. If an extended study of the Spencer canon teaches only one lesson, it is that the human individual is a communal animal. Amos does manage to accumulate land, power, wealth, and some prestige in his crusade into the Delta, but along the way he refuses the support and identity offered by the Dudleys, by Thelma Dubard and Arney Talliafero, by Ary and her niece Dolly, and even by his

---

12. *This Crooked Way* is similar to Shakespeare's dark comedies, such as *Measure for Measure* and *The Winter's Tale,* in a number of interesting ways. In these late plays, Shakespeare typically converts what for four acts appears to be incipient tragedy into comedy in the last act, sometimes by mystical means. In *The Winter's Tale,* he accomplishes this by the apparent return to life of a statue, an appropriate analogy for the recovery of Amos Dudley.

own children. Seen in the light of his amazing successes juxtaposed against his desperate loneliness, Amos is clearly a sort of idiot savant, a man whose strengths are only less breathtaking than his weaknesses. In the closing section he asks himself, "How can a man follow the ways of his heart except by keeping it a secret way? Crooked as it goes and far from home, he must still follow it." As soon as he asks the question, he realizes the answer. He says of Ary that "she had ended" his crooked journey "because as sure as it is true that you can keep people ignorant, you can't keep them harmless, and in finishing out my secret way I had to count on them more than I knew" (226).

What Amos does not realize even at the end is what fate Ary has saved him from. Spencer borrows her title from Chaucer's *Pardoner's Tale,* two lines of which she quotes as epigraph:

> Now, sirs, quod he, if that you be so leef
> To find Deeth, turne up this croked wey.

For forty-five years Amos, in his self-aggrandizing isolation, had chased death without realizing it. The three egotistical idlers of Chaucer's tale destroy one another for money, and the same destination looms at the end of Amos Dudley's crooked way. Late in her indictment, Ary finally admits to Dolly why she fears her husband: "Because I know that he is death. He has to possess and what he possesses he has to destroy. To all that I love, hide it as he will, he is sudden and ruthless death. . . . And why? For me—to move in closer, to destroy, my heart, myself, me. Me utterly. Oh, he is death!" (201–202). Before Ary both breaks and saves him, Amos Dudley is death—potential death to all who love him as well as to himself. His life, both before and after the transformation wrought by the murder, reveals just how dangerous a delusion is self-isolation.

If *Fire in the Morning* introduced Spencer's fundamental concern with the laws of intimacy and community, *This Crooked Way* explicates fully perhaps the most powerful of those laws. No human being can know himself or herself separate from the human community. Marriage, family, community, the threat of the outsider—the same motifs of communion are present in both novels. In her second novel, however, Spencer discovered a way to structure her narrative to reflect her thematic concerns. Amos Dudley's self-obsession fractures the communal lives of those around him into fragments of narration, all of which point toward his impenetrable nature as the missing piece of the puzzle. When Spencer finally disentangles him from God and adds his voice to the chorus, a harmony results. What had appeared as a crooked story indeed becomes instead a circle that takes the reader back to the beginning and so knits up the human fragments in comic communion.

When Amos surrenders his fascination with self-centered godliness, he discovers a true spiritual union in his relations with his wife and family. In this way, the last section of *This Crooked Way* anticipates Spencer's later novels, especially *The Salt Line,* in which spirituality is clearly a function of communion rather than isolation. Although Amos Dudley's first-person revelations confused the novel's original critics, the novel's last section now seems prophetic— both of Spencer's later technical experiments and of her growing interest in the spirituality of community.

3 / Challenging the Forefathers

The segregation that *Voice at the Back Door* explores was really a tenet of faith in the white South before 1940.

To challenge it was to challenge the rightness and righteousness of your forefathers. So, reexamining that whole system was a very personal experience for me.
                                                    —Elizabeth Spencer, in an interview

After the disappointing critical reception of *This Crooked Way,* Spencer published the two novels for which she has become best known—*The Voice at the Back Door* (1956) and *The Light in the Piazza* (1960). Although *The Voice at the Back Door* is more traditional in technique than *This Crooked Way,* its intricate characterization, pared-down style, and suspenseful plot all suggest Spencer's growing ability. Appearing as it did near the beginning of the civil rights movement, its topical treatment of southern race relations drew a large audience, and critics responded with universal approval. The *New Yorker* reviewer called it "a practically perfect novel," and it has remained Spencer's most popular book with the reading public.[1]

In addition to its popularity, it is significant in several ways. It is Spencer's last novel-length portrait of small-town Mississippi life; later novels mirror in their setting Spencer's own removal to a more cosmopolitan existence. It also represents what she has several times described as an exploration of her own feelings about race, specifically the segregated mentality of the Deep South. Written primarily in Italy just before racial tensions exploded across the South, *The Voice at the Back Door* describes perhaps the last moment in American history when race could be considered as a local rather than regional

1. Brendan Gill, "Books: All Praise," *New Yorker,* December 15, 1956, p. 180.

or national issue. This allowed Spencer to confine the novel's action to Lacey, Mississippi, and the surrounding Winfield County, attaining at once a dramatic focus on individual lives and a format for her characteristic attention to community dynamics.

The town of Lacey, Mississippi—based loosely like the earlier Tarsus on Spencer's hometown, Carrollton—is intensely self-aware. It is a town where "no one on the . . . square would have anything but a glass door" through which to study the lives of fellow inhabitants (10). In Lacey even the most intimate relationships are all but public property. Love affairs, like that of the young Duncan Harper and Marcia Mae Hunt, are woven into Lacey's self-image so that an unforeseen marriage or a sudden breakup affects the lives of the townspeople. On many issues, the citizens of Lacey—particularly the white citizens—think and move as one. When an angry audience at a political rally turns into a mob, Marcia Mae Hunt realizes suddenly that the crowd is one dangerous entity. Yet this scene is no more than the actualization of a potential that has existed in Lacey since the opening pages of the novel. The individuals who live in Lacey share a deep well of common history, a communal consciousness that governs most of what they do and think. Ultimately, then, all relationships in Lacey, racial or otherwise, are shaped by public opinion.

The public nature of intimacy in this environment creates an emotional pressure cooker that distorts the lives of its inhabitants: Nan Hunt's migraine headaches, Marcia Mae Hunt's restless desire to escape, Jimmy Tallant's self-destructiveness, as well as the universal social hypocrisy, are all symptoms of a hypersensitive social awareness. Spencer sharply defines the extent of Lacey's hypocrisy when she describes the "sheriff's women." Although he is married to Miss Ada, the quintessential "southern belle" pickled in her own purity, Sheriff Travis Brevard would "rather die in a gully than on her bedspread." He would prefer, he admits to Duncan Harper, to go to Ida Belle, who had been his "nigger woman for fifteen years" and mother of his children (8). As Prenshaw points out, Brevard's dilemma is that of every Lacey resident, "split between public and private selves, between professing and feeling, . . . spiritually homeless" (54).

While Spencer's explicit, even melodramatic, concern is race relations in the South, the underlying theme of the novel has to do with the struggle of the individual—white or black, male or female—to live an honest life in this dangerously flawed society. *The Voice at the Back Door* is in this way the culmination of Spencer's study of small-town Mississippi life.

Sheriff Brevard is a physically imposing man who has for years kept order among both white and black through intimidation. When the novel opens, he is dying. He rushes to the small store owned by Duncan Harper, a former football hero and local legend. He asks Duncan to run for sheriff when he dies, noting that in all the county only Duncan and Jimmy Tallant, a local war hero who is now a bootlegger, have the personality and intelligence to run things. After Brevard's death, Duncan and his friend Tallant come into conflict as Duncan pursues the sheriff's office for two idealistic reasons: to shut down the illegal liquor sales in the county and to guarantee blacks equal rights under the law. Tallant, of course, intends to fight Duncan on the liquor issue despite his promise to Duncan's wife, Tinker, not to oppose him in the open election. Tallant realizes that the "race question" is Duncan's Achilles' heel, that no integrationist could win office in Winfield County.

These public issues are complicated by the fact that Duncan and Tallant are two members of an emotionally charged quartet. Duncan had for years been paired with Marcia Mae Hunt, a local debutante who broke off their engagement suddenly and inexplicably the summer they were to be married. While recovering, Duncan turned to Louise "Tinker" Taylor, who had been involved with Jimmy Tallant. While Tallant was in Europe shooting down twenty-three Nazi planes and earning a place in local folklore, Tinker Taylor became Tinker Harper, creating a whole new set of complications in the lives of these four friends.

Spencer has said in several interviews that her early thinking about the novel focused on two elements. One was the historical event of the courthouse massacre (which was based on a tragedy that occurred in Carrollton) and its place in the collective consciousness of a small Mississippi town. The second was the emotionally charged complex of four characters—Duncan, Tinker, Tallant, and Marcia Mae. When Marcia Mae's sister Cissy remarks jealously, "You were the main ones. Things didn't happen without you" (156), her words are true of the novel as well as of Lacey High School. Almost nothing in the book happens that is not central to, or at least profoundly influenced by, these four lives. The emotional ties—generated by respect as well as love—that bind them together are complex and

deeply rooted; even when they are at odds, as Duncan and Tallant
are through most of the novel, they still understand each other
better than do any other characters. Spencer uses the web of their
relationships to study how private lives and public action are inextricably woven together.

Of these four, Spencer first introduces Duncan Harper. He is a
"shrewd," if quiet man, a former All-American football player who
is so physically self-assured that "he could behave gently" even under
duress (12, 17). Much to the surprise of Travis Brevard and others,
Duncan had returned to Lacey after the war and settled into an
uneventful life as family man and storekeeper. Brevard's death creates
in Duncan a tremor of doubt, a subtle uneasiness about his place in
the scheme of things. He has discussed with Kerney Woolbright
what they hope is the changing social climate of the South, the
postwar relaxation of racial and social tensions. Suddenly faced with
Brevard's demand that he become a leader in the community, Duncan is forced to act on his liberal beliefs. He is appointed sheriff in
anticipation of the general election six months later, and in the
interim, the community at large experiences a crisis brought on by
his idealism. Duncan is so threatening to Lacey because he, unlike
Kerney Woolbright, is an insider, literally the town's "fair-haired
boy," whose character and personality are shaped out of his Lacey
background.

He is, in fact, so self-assured on his home field of Winfield County
that the public anger his beliefs generate is at first not nearly as
threatening to him and his family as his short, private affair with
Marcia Mae Hunt. After the brief rekindling of their desire subsides,
Duncan realizes that "he knew himself by certain things, by their
certain manner of being themselves that identified them with his
deepest self. He wanted, positively now, to go home to his wife and
children" (181). Duncan's homing instinct is more than just familial;
it is communal as well: "Duncan Harper was a citizen of Lacey, that
was it. Just answering a question about love could not alter this fact.
Just saying 'Come away' could not change it. It was his strongest and
final quality" (181).

Duncan has become the individual embodiment of the best that
Lacey can be. He is so much in tune with the community consciousness that though political and racial strife rages around him, he remains a still center in the storm. He accepts the limitations of the
community as his own even as he tries to move the center of its

life by sheer will and personality toward a more honest, more just existence.

That he is the town's best and brightest while remaining so essentially its "citizen" sets the stage for his tragic death. Early in the novel, Tinker Harper explains half-jokingly to Tallant that Kerney and, by extension, Duncan think "the day of the liberal is at hand. . . . All you have to do is get a few people in a few towns to take a great big risk of being martyrs, only it will seem like a bigger risk then it actually is because people know deep down . . . that the old reactionary position of the South has played out to nothing but a lot of sentiment" (29). Tallant knows only too well what the idealistic Duncan fails to see—that the old reactionary position is as entrenched as ever. In threatening the segregationist status quo, Duncan is in danger of becoming a very real martyr to his cause, and finally Spencer uses him in just that way. Like the classical tragic hero, Duncan is a significant figure in his society (chosen by Travis Brevard to reign after him), he personifies his culture while simultaneously rising above it, and he makes choices that set in motion a chain of events that destroys him. He is possessed of a tragic flaw—his betrayal of wife and family for the illicit affections of Marcia Mae Hunt, which, if it does not drive him insane in high classical fashion, does render him more plausible to the reader.[2] As the novel progresses, it becomes obvious that Duncan is so idealistic that he must be sacrificed to his cause. Those who arrived first at "the scene of the [fatal] wreck were rewarded. . . . They . . . heard all the first hand stories—stories that would be good for generations" (305). Duncan Harper, the perfectly communal man, is destined to become the stuff of folklore.

Despite his heroic status, however, Duncan Harper is not the most interesting character in the novel.[3] That role Spencer reserved for Jimmy Tallant, the fighter ace turned bootlegger. Tallant is inti-

2. Spencer told Broadwell and Hoag that Duncan's moral simplicity is also a flaw: "He pushes everything forward to the breaking point. I think that a man who sees things in such simplistic terms—who says, for example, 'this is good and therefore I will do it'—a man like this has a flaw in character. It's a failure in his character that he could never perceive evil." Broadwell and Hoag, "Conversation," in *Conversations with Elizabeth Spencer*, ed. Prenshaw, 62.

3. Spencer admitted as much to Broadwell and Hoag. Although Duncan is "necessary to the book," he is too simple to generate in-depth reflection. "He's not as interesting to me," Spencer said, "as a mixed character like Jimmy Tallant or even Beck Dozer." *Ibid*.

mately connected to the central quartet through his ongoing love for Tinker Harper, Duncan's wife. Early in the novel, he sneaks into the Harpers' house in order to spy on the family for a few minutes before making his presence known. He does so not for political reasons but because "the room that he spied in upon was his favorite in all the world—the place where he cared most to be. That it was another man's living room was ironic, and of this he was all too fully aware." (19). Tallant loved the room because it had been designed, decorated, and lovingly used by Tinker Harper. The irony that Spencer associates with Tallant at this early point foreshadows the fuller portrait to follow—intelligent, articulate, friendly, and aware of the darkly ironic nature of the world. Even though his livelihood depends on the sale of illegal whiskey, he promises Tinker he will not run against Duncan, whom he could easily defeat. Later in the novel, he again offers to sacrifice himself and his way of life to save Beck Dozer when he admits to Duncan that he had been "accidentally" shot by a New Orleans mobster. On the same day he is shot, he lovingly protects the visiting Tinker from being discovered at the roadhouse, again passing up political gain out of personal gallantry. In Tallant, Spencer sketches a knight-errant lost in the modern world. He has become out of necessity a practiced "actor" with a keen sense of when the "joke [was] on Jimmy Tallant" (49, 66). After Duncan's death, he is recruited to run for sheriff as a write-in candidate, his supporters even accepting at face value his defense of Dozer. "I'm not to be trusted," Tallant tells them. "I'm basically unsound," meaning simply that he was not then and never would be who they assumed he was (308).

Jimmy Tallant is Spencer's first great achievement in characterization. Full of complexities, he is seemingly immoral yet deeply romantic, laconic while at the same time flippantly cynical, witty, tough, loyal, and, ultimately, self-destructive. He scorns Duncan Harper, not because he married the woman Tallant loved, but because of Duncan's simplemindedness, his inability to recognize evil. For Tallant is profoundly aware of the human potential for evil as a result of his inherited guilt from the massacre. He is bound up with Beck Dozer in an evolving relationship that suggests the general relationship in the South between white and black. He is driven by a deep sense of frustration and loss. Deprived of Tinker, he marries Bella, the silly, promiscuous daughter of his bootlegging partner, saddling himself with an all-but-unendurable marriage. Threatened by Duncan's candidacy, he subtly stage-manages a confrontation at the jail to publicize Duncan's integrationist tendencies, a stunt that is at the same time a subtle suicide attempt. When he is shot and nearly killed by the innocent young mob gunman, it is the result of his own trickery, again a near-successful suicide attempt. Of all the characters in *The Voice at the Back Door*, Tallant is most aware of the difficult and frustrating ties of guilt and allegiance that bind him. His cynical humor and romantic gallantry are symptoms of his plight. That he survives to be reconciled with Beck Dozer at the end of the novel, that having given up his wife there is the possibility of a reunion with Tinker, that he has replaced illegal liquor with cattle farming—all of these things suggest finally a brighter future for Jimmy Tallant, one the reader feels he has earned. The price he has had to pay for even the possibility of happiness suggests just how confined he is by community.

If Jimmy Tallant is a mercurial, delightfully unpredictable element in *The Voice at the Back Door*, Spencer balances his presence with that of Tinker Harper, Duncan's wife and Tallant's "state of mind" (30). Spencer has said of Tinker: "She is almost a saint figure, a person without worldly interests. Her main concern is to love."[4] She discourages both Duncan and Tallant from getting involved in politics; she tells them that if they "begin running for these little two-by-four courthouse jobs in Winfield County, you're going to fight with each other and have all sorts of grudges. You aren't going to want to come here or anywhere else and talk any more. You aren't even going to want to have a drink together any more" (23).

The course of events proves her right: Duncan and Tallant split over the whiskey issue, and Duncan asks him not to come back to their house until after the election, breaking apart the group before her fireplace that Tinker had most treasured. Because she had been a social misfit in childhood, Tinker's response to the hypocrisy demanded by life in Lacey is to gather around her those she loves in a protective circle. She holds Duncan, Tallant, and her children apart from the rest of the world, desiring only to love and protect them. Hers is a futile desire; in Spencer's world, self-isolation is a dangerous delusion. Tinker's marriage is threatened by Marcia Mae Hunt, and she is cut off from Tallant by politics.

It becomes increasingly obvious to her and to the reader that she

4. *Ibid*.

cannot build a world apart, that she must venture out into a confused and violent society to maintain her ties to those she loves. Estranged from Duncan and desperate for someone to confide in, she visits Tallant at the roadhouse. She is momentarily distracted by his gentle honesty and humor, but they are interrupted first by Bud Grantham, Jimmy's partner, and then by the New Orleans gangsters. What had begun as a relatively innocent visit becomes tragically complicated when Tallant is shot, and because she is still close by, Tinker is the first at his side. This pattern repeats itself on Speaking Day when Duncan gets the message that Beck Dozer is waiting to turn himself in at a country store. By now reconciled with Duncan, Tinker insists on going with him, and this second venture out into the world of personal and political treachery also ends tragically. Tinker herself takes decisive action in defending Duncan and Dozer, but then she is in the car with them when it crashes, killing Duncan.

Early in the novel, three men gather around her hearth. All three love her, and she counsels all three to leave politics to others. But Kerney Woolbright betrays them all including himself, Jimmy Tallant is shot and nearly killed, and her husband dies a violent death. By the end of the book, except for Tallant, the pressures of Lacey society have corrupted or killed her loved ones. Like Tallant, however, she grows in stature through suffering. Although the world forces her to realize she cannot protect her chosen few, she continues to answer treachery with love.

Marcia Mae Hunt's answer to the pressures of Lacey communal life contrasts sharply with Tinker Harper's. Whereas Tinker chose to marry Duncan and try to build a haven within Lacey, Marcia Mae broke up with Duncan and sought a simpler identity elsewhere. After marrying the first attractive man she meets because "he had no consciousness of families, small towns, roots, ties, or any sort of custom," she loses interest in him for the same reason (174). When he is killed in the war, she inexplicably returns to Lacey, only later realizing that she has come back "to tell [Duncan] everything," to try yet one more time to explain why she had left (160).

She had been forced to leave, she explains, because in the tautly self-conscious world of Lacey, their lives had been laid out for them from childhood. "We couldn't stay in the South and be free," she tells Duncan. "We couldn't breath even until we left" (171). Duncan, however, is too much a contextual creature to understand her objections. He has so thoroughly accepted their prescribed lives that he cannot follow her. Even after her return, Marcia Mae tells Duncan and Kerney that she would prefer total anonymity to a role assigned her by Lacey: "I wish . . . that I was anybody's secretary in some big city. And that every morning I got up and put on a gray suit and a clean white blouse and went to work in a beautiful soundproof air-conditioned office one hundred and one floors up, with stream-lined filing cabinets and a noiseless electric typewriter. I wish I had a little apartment with a view from the window of nothing but skyscraper tops. Then I would be happy" (109). She desires the freedom of anonymity, the exact opposite of life in Lacey. Although she is unable for the second time to convince Duncan to leave with her, she remains loyal to him, trying to warn him against the Speaking Day crowd as a final gesture of affection.

Marcia Mae realizes more clearly than any other character in the novel how strictly the small southern town governs the actions of its citizens. Even white males are constrained by social, racial, and gender distinctions. Marcia Mae's brother, for example, had died torturing himself over his homosexuality, and it takes Jimmy Tallant's brush with death before he will openly befriend Beck Dozer.[5] Even though she has been given the lead role in Lacey's social drama (twice college homecoming queen), Marcia Mae instinctively recoils from the constraints she sees ruining her mother and her sister. Chief among the small town's weapons, she tells Duncan, is family. "In the South, it's nothing but family, family. We [can't] breathe even" (171). The best illustration of this social pressure comes during their first chance meeting in front of the Lacey post office. In the town's communal consciousness they are an indissoluble pair despite their marriages to others: "She had parked her convertible, gathered up her bag and gloves and had one foot out of the door when she saw him, and knew she could not turn back. The square seemed empty, but she knew from old experience that it was not. In Lacey someone was always watching, and by no means could she lack courage"(32).

She and Duncan are, in other words, on stage, and their sense of being watched frustrates even their secret rendezvous. Marcia Mae

5. Prenshaw's emphasis on the dilemma of the southern woman has a lot of merit. But *all* the inhabitants of Spencer's Lacey face severe difficulties in "reconciling heart's desire with social reality" unless, like Duncan Harper, they fit their assigned roles naturally. To suggest "that the chance of an independent woman's finding fulfillment in the South of the 1950's was even less likely than that of a black man's doing so" overstates the case. Prenshaw, *Elizabeth Spencer*, 58.

tells Duncan she feels no guilt that is not imposed on her from
without: "I feel that other people are trying to make me say I'm
wrong whether I think so or not. I've always hated that about Lacey.
They all know how right they are. Anybody who disagrees is wrong.
Why shouldn't I see you? Who else is there in the world I'd want
to talk to? If we want to meet for dinner right uptown in the cafe
and sit there till closing time, whose business is it to have any opinion
about it?" (164–65).

Duncan, on the other hand, does feel an internalized guilt, and
it is this difference, leading to his refusal to leave with her, which
eventually breaks them apart. Marcia Mae, like Randall Gibson in
Fire in the Morning, abhors a life so strictly defined by community,
a life lived in so public an arena. Even before Duncan's death, she
senses that she will again leave Lacey, this time for good.

Spencer places these four characters at the core of the novel to
illustrate how public, communal life and private, intimate life are
intertwined. Confronted by Duncan Harper over the "race issue,"
Jimmy Tallant twists the argument around to the topic of Tinker.
"Every time I said, who do you love? she said Duncan," he com-
plains. Duncan's response is significant.

"It's true things never worked out for us the way we thought they
would," Duncan said earnestly. "But what's done is done. I don't think our
private lives should have anything to do with the nigger in the jail, or the
bootlegging business, or the sheriff's race. I think you've got to face public
things in another frame of mind."

"My father did a public thing," said Jimmy Tallant. "He shot Robinson
Dozer, among others, and that's Dozer's son that's sitting in the jail house.
You'd be surprised how private it makes me feel." (97)

The inseparability that Jimmy Tallant senses between the public and
the private is a central concern of this and nearly all of Spencer's
fiction. Duncan's moralizing on the subject is patently naïve. In
Spencer's world, public and private life are one unbroken emotional
and psychological continuum; those who pretend otherwise do so
out of ignorance and at their own risk. Even Duncan is forced to
recognize this when, at a crucial point near the end of the novel, he
tells Beck Dozer to get into the front seat of his car. He does so in
front of two white drifters, and nothing he has done to this point
is as dangerous. In Lacey's superheated social atmosphere, even the
slightest gesture is politically significant, and even the most public
act causes private repercussions. To realize this theme across a full

cultural and racial canvas, however, Spencer needed more than these four central figures. She needed the ambitious Kerney Woolbright and the enigmatic Beckwith Dozer.

Although he was raised in Mississippi, Kerney Woolbright is not from Lacey, and his years at Yale Law School have blunted his instincts about the local social institutions. If ignorant of the local ways, he is blatantly ambitious; his courtship of Cissy Hunt is calculated to win the support of her father, Jason, a retired Lacey businessman. Although he is accepted in the Harper home, neither Duncan nor Jimmy Tallant takes him seriously. At one point he tries half-seriously to start an argument between the two, and Tallant calls his bluff. "Junior," says Tallant, "just because they give you a drink of whisky, it's no sign you can shoot the twelve-gauge or borrow the car" (22). Even the generous Tinker notes to herself that "he did seem so young when he came out with things like this" (25). Kerney Woolbright, however, is destined to flourish in the slippery arena of Lacey politics. On the night of Duncan's confrontation at the jail with Tallant and the Granthams, Woolbright promises Duncan to hurry to join him and then watches the outcome secretly from a parked car. Spencer establishes his cowardice here to prepare the reader for his public betrayal of Duncan at the Speaking. By late in the novel, he has become a disciple of the cynical Jason Hunt and is willing to bend any law, private or public, for the sake of his political reputation. Kerney, as Tinker tells Duncan after Woolbright's segregationist speech, has begun to care "too much" what the ignorant voters think (268).

On the day of the Speaking, Duncan is expecting a telegram from New Orleans that will clear Beck Dozer of Tallant's shooting and so relieve his candidacy of a number of its racial liabilities. The telegram is delivered to Woolbright, who intentionally pockets it, robbing Duncan of the information he needs. When, after Woolbright's speech, Cissy Hunt innocently glances at the telegram, Woolbright is horrified. In a chapter ironically entitled "The Public Man," he drives Cissy to an isolated spot and then proceeds, for the first time, to seduce her. Immediately afterward, he asks her if she will tell.

"Tell? Oh, they'd never let us back together if I told."
"I mean the telegram."
The telegram [to her] was like a stray piece of paper washing up and down in the ocean.

> "I don't care about it," she said.
> He raised his head. "But I do."
> His hand moved through her hair again, caressing and firm.
> "Then I won't. I won't tell. Never, never." (275–76)

By the time they return to the Hunts, they are engaged—she committed by the sexual act, he by the need for secrecy. He has attacked the last bastion of Cissy Hunt's prissiness not out of love or passion but out of fear for his political reputation. His public betrayal of Duncan Harper is mirrored on the same day by his intimate betrayal of Cissy Hunt. After Duncan's death, he is obsessed with guilt and loss. The last paragraph of the novel portrays him outside Tinker Harper's house, "crying aloud with great innocent sobs, like a little boy" (326). Although he has won his treasured election, he remains in Spencer's eyes a vicious child.

Cissy Hunt, Woolbright's willing victim, is for most of the novel blissfully uninterested in politics. She flirts disdainfully with Woolbright, marveling at his social simplemindedness. After his Speaking Day performance, she chastises Marcia Mae for condemning Kerney.

> "You mean you're not going to let him ride home because of something he said in a speech? That's the silliest thing I ever heard of."
> "You mean to say you are? Don't you know he just stabbed his best friend in the back? Publicly?"
> "I don't understand anything about it and neither do you. You always want to make a big fuss." (273)

She is silly, prissy, whining, trading on her supposed naïveté—until she has sex with Woolbright. After Duncan's death, her new fiancé is approached by her father about the telegram, and before Kerney can even speak, she defends him so adeptly that her father accepts Kerney's lie at face value. What happened in Kerney's car after the speeches accomplished what his political rhetoric could not. It transformed Cissy Hunt into a political animal. Here again, Spencer manipulates plot materials to stress the subtle connection between public and private worlds.

Another, even subtler, example of the same connection is Beckwith Dozer's personal fight for equal rights juxtaposed against his relationship with Jimmy Tallant. Dozer is a war veteran who has seen too much of the world to return to a Winfield County passivity. Despite this, however, he helps Tallant frame Harper as a "nigger lover," explaining to Harper later that he does not "run in pack" with anybody and that he prefers the status quo: "You can climb the status quo like a step ladder with two feet on the floor, but trying to trail along behind a white man of good will is like following behind somebody on a tightrope. As he gets along towards the middle his problems are likely to increase, and soon he gots to turn loose of me to help himself" (122–23).

When Duncan reminds him that he has protected Dozer in good faith, however, Dozer gives in and agrees to help him expose Tallant's plot. Spencer has said that Beck's "is the theme of emergence," that he is "ambivalent because he was entering a new era of his own culture."[6] It is also true, however, that Beck's actions are inconsistent because he responds to personal appeal and affection as well as racial duty. As with many of Spencer's best characters, his complexity stems from the conflict between self-identity and community, in this instance racial community. Ironically, the personal bond to which he is most responsive is the complex one he shares with Jimmy Tallant.

The two are mysteriously bound by their shared past, by the murder of Dozer's father by Tallant's. Tallant's suicidal tendencies are at least partly the result of his inherited guilt, an Old Testament case of the sins of the father being visited on the son. During the war, Dozer played on Tallant's guilt to nearly arrange his death. As Tallant tells his wife, he used to brag cynically to British soldiers about his daddy shooting "twelve niggers dead in one afternoon between two and two-fifteen." He continues: "One night in a pub during the buzz-bomb raid, I said those words . . . and . . . a voice a whole lot flatter than mine said, 'It's the truth. His daddy shot them dead.' I said, 'Where you from and what's your name?' . . . 'My name is Sergeant Beckwith Dozer.' Then everybody hit for cover because it was going to be a near one, and just when the silence came I walked to the door and outside" (67).

Tallant is nearly killed in the explosion, and the next time he sees Dozer, they are "on the Lacey square and the war was over. But he remembered and I did too, and the bastard grinned, remembering the time he nearly killed me" (67). This experience intensifies what is already a significant mutual awareness, and by the time of Duncan Harper's campaign for sheriff, they have become partners. Beck tells

6. Broadwell and Hoag, "Conversation," in *Conversations with Elizabeth Spencer,* ed. Prenshaw, 63.

Duncan: "Mister Tallant and I are tied together on account of what his daddy did to mine. He wouldn't lose me, nor let me come to harm for anything in the world. He's my main protection in this life. That and he pays me for what he gets me to do" (122).

After Tallant is shot by the New Orleans gangster, he risks first his business interests in order to protect Dozer from suspicion and then finally his own life when he escorts Dozer away from the scene of Duncan's fatal accident. Spencer returns to the pair—white and black—once more in the novel, in the last chapter before the epilogue. They are sitting in the roadhouse parking lot when a car pulls up and a voice offers Tallant the opportunity to be elected sheriff as a write-in; he refuses out of disgust, telling the men he now favors "equal rights" (308–309). In Spencer's South, white and black are indissolubly connected by common history and common blood.

In fact, the novel subtly highlights one of the central ironies of southern segregation. An artificially divided society such as that of the Jim Crow South only forces each segment of the community to be hypersensitive to the other. In Spencer's Mississippi, as well as the South at large, whites and blacks have history in common as well as blood. When Duncan Harper sees Robinson Dozer's portrait hanging in Beck Dozer's house, the whole story leading up to and including the courthouse massacre flashes involuntarily through his mind. When he turns back to Lucy Dozer, "each in their own way knew the whole story, but whether they had been told it or not or by whom would never be clear. Southerners hear parts of stories with their ears, and the rest they know with their hearts" (226). The massacre is a "core event" in Lacey history—equally intense for black and white. Duncan Harper's martyrdom is destined to become an event of equal historical intensity. After the accident, Dozer tells Jimmy Tallant that he spends "every waking hour thinking on that wreck. . . . I think and think, and what I always ask is, 'Why him? If somebody had to die, why wasn't it me?' " Tallant tries to dispel Dozer's mood by saying: "It just happened that way. There's nothing to wonder about" (310). But even he has been profoundly affected by Duncan's death: "It was perhaps the first time in his life he had ever thought or spoken of Duncan without a lurking scorn" (311). Duncan's death has raised his life out of the personal realm into that of community legend. Spencer sacrifices him to Lacey's bigotry, setting in motion the erosion of that bigotry, as witnessed in Jimmy Tallant. Harper's public sacrifice accomplishes what neither his public nor private life could; it erases Tallant's guilt and leaves him believing in "equal rights."

Spencer uses the twelve-page epilogue to trace the effect of Duncan's death in the rest of the community. Even those who barely knew him are affected as his passing begins to sink into the collective consciousness that is Lacey: "For in [a] small town, in a society whose supreme interest is people, the past exists physically—empty chairs expect the dead and not in vain" (256). The community, much like an individual character, has an all but palpable past, out of which the present is constantly evolving. Duncan Harper, in being the first to openly advocate equality and for no other reason than its essential rightness, has altered the identity of the entire community. In becoming part of their past, he has become a part of their perpetual present.

The Voice at the Back Door is Spencer's most detailed, most comprehensive study of the small southern town that is her heritage as a writer. Ironically, it was written in Italy, where Spencer returned after its publication in 1956. She then began to apply the sensibility and talent honed in small southern communities to a much larger, and in some ways even more complicated, social landscape. Her next two novellas, *The Light in the Piazza* and *Knights and Dragons,* are both set in Italy, and both deal with the emotional and psychological trials of an American woman in an alien environment. These two works signal an important turning point for Spencer. From international alienation, she turned to a fictional study of America as a cultural community, the scope of her work growing ever larger. No matter how expansive her canvas, however, she never abandoned the themes she first studied in the three Mississippi novels.

4 / *Italy: Dream and Nightmare*

Nobody with a dream should come to Italy. No matter how dead and buried the dream is thought to be, in Italy it will rise and walk again.
— *The Light in the Piazza*

Although its popularity has not lasted, *The Light in the Piazza* was even more immediately successful than *The Voice at the Back Door*. Peggy Prenshaw has described in some detail how, in addition to a McGraw-Hill Fiction Award, *The Light in the Piazza* received rave reviews. For example, Orville Prescott (New York *Times*) thought it "one of the four or five best novels of 1960"; Susan M. Black (*New Republic*) found it "the best new novel . . . this year"; and Phoebe Adams (*Atlantic Monthly*) praised Spencer's "flawlessly precise choice of words."[1] This immediate success was followed by an MGM movie contract, and Spencer's reputation soared.

The Light in the Piazza is the first of Spencer's books set outside Mississippi and the first to focus primarily on a woman. Both it and the novella that followed five years later, *Knights and Dragons,* are set in Italy and have as their protagonists expatriate American women. Italy causes both these women, Margaret Johnson in *The Light in the Piazza* and Martha Ingram of *Knights and Dragons,* to confront their deepest dreams and fantasies and to engineer drastic changes in their emotional lives. Although a cursory reading of the two might suggest

1. Orville Prescott, "Books of the Times," New York *Times*, November 21, 1960, p. 27; Susan M. Black, "A Dream in Italy," *New Republic,* December 5, 1960, p. 20; Phoebe Adams, Review of Elizabeth Spencer's *The Light in the Piazza* in *Atlantic Monthly,* CCVII (February, 1961), 113; all cited in Prenshaw, *Elizabeth Spencer,* 76.

that together they represent a new departure for Spencer as a novelist, in reality the differences between the two are more important than the similarities. Despite its setting, *The Light in the Piazza* is more like the three Mississippi novels that came before than it is the second Italian novella, *Knights and Dragons*. The evolution in Spencer's methods between the two is more profound than a simple change in setting; comparison reveals significant changes in technique that foreshadow the novels that follow.

The Light in the Piazza is traditionally realistic. Spencer narrates Margaret Johnson's story from a point of limited omniscience associated with Margaret's personality. Despite this technique, the factual realities of Spencer's fictionalized Florence are quite stable; Spencer resolves the mysteries of cultural differences authoritatively. In *Knights and Dragons,* she treats the same setting with basically the same narrative technique but to a much different end. She still limits the omniscience of her third-person point of view largely to the mind of her protagonist, but in this case, the result is a surreal world. Factual reality in *Knights and Dragons* has become less significant as it has become less verifiable. Spencer studies the evolution of Martha Ingram's emotional and psychological life by focusing on the way her perceptions of the world, both real and imagined, develop and by using various characters and situations allegorically to represent her emotional state. Spencer experiments with several difficult techniques in *Knights and Dragons* in an effort to develop a method for exploring the effect of communal stress on the individual personality. A comparison of *The Light in the Piazza* with *Knights and Dragons* reveals the technical changes Spencer made to transfer her reader's attention from the external world of her characters to the internal.

This new emphasis on the psychology of alienation is a logical outgrowth of Spencer's fascination with community dynamics. It also foreshadows the themes and techniques of the novels she has written since *Knights and Dragons*: *No Place for an Angel, The Snare, The Salt Line,* and *The Night Travellers*. All four of these novels are more immediately accessible than *Knights and Dragons* because in each Spencer establishes a viable plot as an external correlative to the internal evolution of her characters. Before she could write any of these later books, however, she had to take the technical risks of *Knights and Dragons*. She had to make the artistic leap of faith from the more traditional, well-lighted world of *The Light in the Piazza* to the "devious stairways, corridors, and cortili" of *Knights and Drag-ons.*[2] Unfortunately, contemporary reviewers did not take kindly to Spencer's artistic experiments. Orville Prescott (who had praised *The Light in the Piazza*) and Stanley Kauffmann (*New Republic*) strongly challenged Spencer's shift in emphasis.[3]

To have elicited such disparate responses, the story lines of the two novellas are actually quite similar. In *The Light in the Piazza*, Margaret Johnson and her daughter Clara are traveling in Italy. Because of a childhood accident, Clara has in many ways the mental age of eight or ten. Realizing in Italy that Clara is capable of a traditional Italian marriage, a role that will require nothing more of her than inno-cence, devotion, and fertility, Mrs. Johnson decides to arrange it for her. In so doing, she overcomes two difficulties: the doubts of the groom's father and her own husband's potential objections. After both managing Clara's intricate marriage negotiations and mentally answering her internalized image of her husband, Margaret Johnson emerges from her time in Italy with a new confidence both in her intelligence and her sexuality.

The plot of *Knights and Dragons* is less compelling, however. Because Martha Ingram, Spencer's protagonist, is a dangerously wounded sensibility, the view of Italy the reader receives through her is distorted. Physical details are often vague or altogether absent, but it is clear that Martha Ingram has come to Italy to escape. She was married for a number of years to Gordon Ingram, an older man and famous scholar, but their marriage devolved into an emotional nightmare, and she fled the States for Italy. In seeking to escape her own psychological dragon, her husband, she turns to two potential knights: Jim Wilbourne, a traveling American economist who be-comes her lover, and George Hartwell, her sympathetic boss and confidant. Ultimately, however, neither man can help her, and she must rely on her own instincts to create for herself an emotional independence.

But these two novellas share more than just surface characteristics. Both portray American women who face an emotional crisis while

2. Elizabeth Spencer, *Knights and Dragons* (New York, 1965), 8. Hereinafter cited by page number in the text.

3. Orville Prescott, "Books of the Times: All Aggravation and Ambiguity," New York *Times,* June 30, 1965, p. 35; Stanley Kauffmann, "Sense and Sensibility," *New Republic,* June 26, 1965, pp. 27–28.

isolated from their native communities. Both women must overcome their reluctance to think, feel, and act counter to the wishes
of male authority figures who, though they remain physically in
America, live vividly in the protagonists' minds. Both women fight
the internalized influence of these "dragons" to gain self-possession
and self-direction, and both do so by forming relationships with
men in Italy. In neither book does the absent father-husband figure
actually appear; in each case his influence is entirely internalized.
Neither of the two protagonists, Margaret Johnson or Martha Ingram, win permanent self-control in a healthy sense. Spencer herself
has said that in her writing during this period, she "searched for
women who could sustain a weight of experience, both intellectual
and emotional. I think that often the women characters I found did
not do this. For example Margaret Johnson's triumph was . . . a
fantasy that could explode five minutes after the book was over.
Then Martha Ingram . . . had a weakness in her nature that kept her
from throwing off her obsession [with her former husband]."[4]

Despite their failures, however, each of these women does manage to manipulate the alien world around her to promote her own
emotional healing and eventual self-expression. Each, as Spencer
wrote of Margaret Johnson, "played single-handed and unadvised a
tricky game in a foreign country" and won for herself the ability to
live more freely.[5]

In addition to these similarities in character and situation, Spencer
also chose to narrate the stories in much the same way. She manipulates her limited omniscient point of view to emphasize the inner
development first of Margaret Johnson and then of Martha Ingram.
She shifts the center of consciousness away from the protagonist only
briefly in each and then only late in the piece when the general focus
is well established. Part of the reason for this consistency in point of
view is the primacy of each woman's fantasy life. As Margaret Johnson realizes halfway through *The Light in the Piazza*: "Nobody with
a dream should come to Italy. No matter how dead and buried the
dream is thought to be, in Italy it will rise and walk again" (61).
Margaret Johnson's dream is to find for her retarded daughter a
normal life, and to do so she must overcome the internalized skepti-

4. Broadwell and Hoag, "Conversation," in *Conversations with Elizabeth Spencer,*
ed. Prenshaw, 75.

5. Elizabeth Spencer, *The Light in the Piazza* (New York, 1960), 107. Hereinafter
cited by page number in the text.

cism of her husband. Martha Ingram's dream is to sever herself completely from her former husband, not only to forget her life with him, but also "to be forgotten" by him and his friends (88). Both women have within them images of male authority figures—husbands who have shaped and trained them, figurative fathers to whom they feel they must answer—and they both dream of breaking free of the male dominance they have internalized. In order to dramatize these two internal struggles for psychic freedom, Spencer found it necessary to place the reader's point of view close to the action—largely within the women themselves.

The similarity in narrative technique is compounded by further similarities in psychology. In deciding finally to promote a young Italian's courtship of her daughter Clara, Margaret Johnson departs on a dangerous inner quest as well as a tricky marriage negotiation. When, several years earlier, she had tried—with disastrous results—to arrange a normal school life for Clara, both she and her husband decided she had gone temporarily "out of [her] mind, insane" (64). When the social and cultural rituals leading up to Clara's engagement reach a critical level, Mrs. Johnson draws into herself in order to try to vanquish the nagging doubts buried there by her husband's eminently businesslike manner. "Never before had it seemed so crucial that she see him clearly. What was the truth about him?" (80). She imagines his first stunned reaction after their transatlantic phone conversation, then his relief when his thoughts would turn to the question of the dowry, something to fasten his business acumen to. "She could tell almost to a T, no crystal-ball gazing required," the process he would follow in accepting the bits of information she carefully fed him (82). But she does not face this internalized vision of her husband alone. She has, to distract and inspire her, a complex relationship with Signor Naccarelli, the father of Clara's fiancé and an attractive blend of cynical romanticism. They engage in a season of flirtation mixed inextricably with negotiation, "all an affair for juggling, circling, balancing, very much to his liking," and to Mrs. Johnson's surprise, hers as well (65). While they never quite approach "middle-aged adultery" ("It was a relief [to her] to know that sin was not expected of them" [69]), they are each attracted to the other, and each seeks to use the attraction to gain an advantage in deciding Clara's dowry. Titillated by her own Italian romance, Mrs. Johnson turns back toward her husband after Clara's marriage, wondering "what sort of life, what degree of delight in it, they might . . .

discover . . . together" (109). She has grown while in Italy to a new psychological independence that frees her to regard her husband from an affectionate emotional distance.

Like Margaret Johnson, Martha Ingram is also engaged in a dangerous inner battle. And like Mrs. Johnson, she approaches insanity. Sure that she has seen her former husband, a well-known scholar, in Venice, she reports the sighting matter-of-factly to her confidant.

> "Venice! Your husband was not in Venice," Hartwell corrected her, with a slightly chilly feeling. . . .
> "You see how crazy I am," she pointed out.
> After some time, Hartwell said, "Intentionally crazy, I take it?"
> "It's necessary," she finally replied. (74)

It is necessary because everyone else who knows her former husband thinks him a charming man, universally kind and caring. Only Martha knows what a tyranny his benevolence had become within their home. His image, as well as his constant letters and messengers, haunt her even after several years in Rome:"Sometimes the large figure with the shaggy head left her alone and she would be fine, and then she would get a letter from a lawyer she'd never heard of . . . or an envelope addressed in a black scrawl . . . [or] some admirer of his would come to Rome and say . . . would she please consider. . . . Then she would be unsteady for a week or two" (5–6).

In trying to escape the fear and hatred that remain from her marriage, she takes an unlikely lover, a taciturn American economist. Following almost the same pattern as Margaret Johnson, she uses this relationship to cleanse herself of the psychic dependence and fear she has internalized during her ten-year marriage to Gordon Ingram. When her friend Hartwell questions her about Wilbourne after the affair has ended, she admits that "he only existed in relation to Gordon," thinking to herself that "there had always been the three of them . . . stuck in the same frame" (126). She has used Wilbourne to erase the afterimage of Gordon Ingram, leaving her "not [caring] very deeply about anything, the emotional target she had once plainly furnished [having] disappeared" (168). Like Margaret Johnson, she gains a new independence; however, unlike Margaret, she frees herself of the need for *any* human contact.

Despite these similarities in setting, characterization, and point of view, *The Light in the Piazza* and *Knights and Dragons* are radically different works. *The Light in the Piazza* is a social comedy, a send-up of often inept American tourists adrift in a comic opera culture—or, as Spencer puts it, "a little tall talk to satirize Florence."[6] Although there are ominous notes sounded throughout that remind the reader of the potential dangers of Mrs. Johnson's hopes for Clara, Spencer spins her novella largely out of light-soaked landscapes and social irony. *Knights and Dragons,* on the other hand, is a darkly psychological tale, full of twists and turns that can leave the reader as confused as Martha Ingram herself. Despite some comic moments, Spencer chillingly renders Martha's brush with madness, and her triumph over her former husband is one of desperate abdication rather than victorious manipulation. Whereas *The Light in the Piazza* is consistently realistic, *Knights and Dragons* is often quite surreal. The world as Spencer describes it is as fractured, clouded, and distorted as Martha Ingram's awareness of it. Spencer often has the other characters in the novel do and say what they do for allegorical reasons rather than to advance the plot. Rather than suspenseful action, *Knights and Dragons* offers surreal imagery and seemingly disconnected, evocative dialogue.[7] The differences between the two are so profound that the formula that brought *The Light in the Piazza* instantaneous critical success and popularity failed almost as completely in *Knights and Dragons.* As Prenshaw notes, the novella "was widely reviewed and, with a few . . . exceptions . . . panned by the critics."[8]

Clearly what disappointed the reviewers was the lack of what Orville Prescott in the New York *Times* termed "flesh and blood."[9] The heroine of *The Light in the Piazza* struggles to create unity and order, to bring people together in a realistic "flesh and blood" world. There is a clearly plotted external line of action to complement Margaret's internal struggles to free herself. Martha Ingram, on the other hand, seeks to extricate herself from human relations, using Wilbourne's physical presence only to exorcise Gordon Ingram's psychological one. Even though Spencer does shift the point of view

6. Broadwell and Hoag, "Conversation," in *Conversations with Elizabeth Spencer,* ed. Prenshaw, 67.

7. This may explain why Spencer continues to think of *Knights and Dragons* as a long story rather than a short novel. Although the original edition is fifty-nine pages longer than that of *The Light in the Piazza,* she included it but not the shorter piece in her 1981 volume of collected stories.

8. Prenshaw, *Elizabeth Spencer,* 87.

9. Prescott, "All Aggravation and Ambiguity," 35.

briefly to follow Wilbourne or George Hartwell, neither of the two men becomes more than a friendly pawn in Martha's mental struggles. A more detailed survey of the subtle contrasts between the two novellas reveals just how profound an artistic change of direction these two texts represent.

The first and perhaps most obvious contrast between the two is the relationship each protagonist has with her distant husband. Margaret Johnson's imagined negotiations with her husband suggest that he has taken on the role more of an authoritarian father to his wife than of an agreeable lover and companion. As a businessman and self-made authority, Noel Johnson has ruled their lives in Winston-Salem, North Carolina, but away from his direct influence, Margaret Johnson is free to dream. And in dreaming for Clara, she is caught up in a delightfully ambiguous flirtation with the worldly Signor Naccarelli. Her confidence in her sexual allure and social intelligence grows as she juggles her delicate relations with the Naccarellis. When she finally decides that she can manage quite well without her husband, Spencer describes the moment in terms of a self-revelation: "What is it, to reach a decision? It is like walking down a long Florentine street where, at the very end, a dim shape is waiting until you get there. When Mrs. Johnson finally reached this street and saw what was ahead, she moved steadily forward to see it at long last up close. What was it? Well, nothing monstrous, it seemed; but human, with a face much like her own, that of a woman who loved her daughter and longed for her happiness" (86). She undergoes a personal rejuvenation as a result of her independent action. Flushed with her new strength, she begins to look forward to her reunion with her husband, whereas before she had dreaded it.

Unlike Margaret Johnson, Martha Ingram's dream is to withdraw from a world whose primary emotional figure has victimized her. What had seemed an idyllic marriage to an intriguing older man had turned into an emotional nightmare, the aftereffects of which she could not escape: "She was intellectually as well as emotionally tenacious and she had, furthermore, her question to address to the sky: how can love, in the first place, turn into hate, and how can I, so trapped in hatred, not suffer for it?" (9). She, unlike Margaret Johnson, has no interest in reestablishing relations with her former husband; she wishes, on the contrary, to obliterate him from her mind. In the middle of an emotional encounter with Jim Wilbourne, she blurts out for no apparent reason that "hatred is too much for me. I can't face it; you have to believe that" (59). She is capable neither of bearing her ex-husband's hatred—whether real or imagined— nor of hating him enough to eradicate him from her psyche. She dreams of somehow forgetting the ten years she spent with him or, conversely, as she tells one of his lawyers, wants "only . . . to be forgotten" (88). She has slipped easily into Italian society, taking on the new language and culture like a cloak, and has become a valued employee of the American consul in Rome. She accepts the support- ive friendship of her boss, George Hartwell, and takes as a lover a married American economist on cultural exchange, all in an effort to rid herself of her psychological dragon. She is like Margaret John- son in that she, too, succeeds in her quest; however, she is most unlike her in that the result is emotional "dissolution" (169).

The second and subtler difference between the two Italian novel- las has to do with the degree to which each is structured by an accessible plot. Undoubtedly what generated such immediate success for *The Light in the Piazza* was Spencer's skillful interweaving of external action with Mrs. Johnson's internal development. The plot is engaging and suspenseful, and the setting's exotic depth colorfully rendered. After Mrs. Johnson has let the romance develop for several indecisive weeks, she and Clara receive together a box of "remark- able flowers . . . a species of lily apparently highly regarded" in Italy (53–54). The card reads only NACCARELLI, leaving some doubt as to whether father or son or both have sent them. Mrs. Johnson notices immediately "their enormous naked stamens, based in a back- curling, waxen petal, [and] they struck her as being rather blatantly phallic" (54). This hint of the sexuality lurking between the Naccar- ellis and Clara and herself sends Mrs. Johnson reeling into unchar- acteristic desperation. She lies "wildly" to Clara about an imaginary illness and rushes her away to Rome. In the several weeks of their enforced absence, however, Mrs. Johnson reconsiders, facing in her mind the image of her husband. By the time of their return, she has grown considerably in self-confidence: "As the train drew into the station [at Florence], she felt her blood race, her whole being straighten and poise, to the fine alertness of a drawn bow. Whether Florence knew it or not, she invaded it" (64). In this way Spencer weaves together attitude and action, private mediation and sensibil- ity, with social, even sexual behavior.

The world of *Knights and Dragons,* on the other hand, is not nearly so accessible. While Spencer's study of an evolving personality is even more detailed and sophisticated, the external world that we view through that personality is not as compelling. Because Martha Ingram, Spencer's protagonist, is a dangerously wounded sensibility, the view of Italy the reader receives through her is distorted. Physical details are often vague or altogether absent; factual information that is verified by Spencer's omniscient authority in *The Light in the Piazza* proves slippery in *Knights and Dragons*. As Spencer moves the center of the narrative consciousness deeper into her protagonist's personality, the external world becomes both less significant and less clear.

Yet ultimately, *Knights and Dragons* is a fiction of architectural as well as emotional interiors. For it is in this book that Spencer first experiments with what will become one of the trademarks of her fiction—the use of architectural interiors (and later landscapes) to suggest emotional states. In *Knights and Dragons*, even the cityscape is subsumed within the primary focus on Martha Ingram's internal development. For example, her life as Gordon Ingram's wife is suggested by his apartment: "In . . . the expensive, oak-panelled, high-ceilinged place in New York's upper Seventies, crusted with books and littered with ash trays, she had lived out a life of corners, and tiny chores had lengthened before her like shadows drawn out into a sunslant; . . . there had been the long rainy afternoons, the kindness of the porter, the illness of the dog, the thin slashing of the brass elevator doors, the walks in the park. She still felt small in doorways" (9).

From an existence as one of Gordon Ingram's disciples/house plants she has escaped to Italy, where she again buries herself deep in an apartment building, this time in Rome, where she hides from her previously public life. "She entered her . . . apartment through all the devious stairways, corridors, and cortili that led to it. 'Sequestered,' George Hartwell called her" (8). Embarking on an all but silent affair with the ubiquitous Wilbourne, she meets him secretly at a series of mysterious addresses.

There were streets she'd never heard of, areas she did not know existed, bare-swept rooms at the tops of narrow stairs, the murmur of apartment life from some other floor or some distance back of this one, the sounds of the street. The wires of small electric stoves glowed across the dim twilights of these rooms, and if she reached them first, she would sit quietly waiting for him to come, drawing the heater close to warm her damp feet . . . but when the door opened she would scarcely look up, if at all, and he on his part gave her scarcely more than a passing glance, turning almost at once to put his coat up. (104)

Although their meetings are passionate, "absolute and profound" (104), they are incapable of normal communication: "Reflecting, she was not long in coming upon the truth the little rooms made plain: that they had struck a bargain that lay deeply below the level of ordinary speech" (108). Unlike the aptly named *Light in the Piazza*, what action there is in *Knights and Dragons* takes place almost exclusively indoors, figuratively suggesting the psychological nature of the tale.

Even simple human interaction in this novella takes place at a level below that of normal conversation. When Jim Wilbourne refers mistakenly to her husband early in the book, it rocks Martha Ingram to her core. She tried "to grow gentle once more after the turmoil, the anguish, which his outlandish mental leap at her had, like a depth charge, brought boiling up inside her" (29). Martha's emotional vulnerability stems from her impossible desire to escape a figure that exists solely inside her. After she and Wilbourne become lovers, he tells her that when they first met, she had "seemed . . . enclosed" (56). She is enclosed by her preoccupations with her inner struggles. The passionate bargain that she eventually strikes with Wilbourne can succeed only if it lies "deeply below the level of ordinary speech" because it is there that she needs to be healed.

In portraying Martha Ingram's psychological quest in all its intensity and complexity, Spencer sacrifices what suspense and drama she might have generated with a more externalized plot. There is ample proof that she is aware of the gamble she is taking in the way she intentionally refuses to verify a single version of external events. When they first meet, Wilbourne mistakenly assumes Martha is the former wife of an acquaintance and tells her that her ex-husband was wounded in a hunting accident. Seriously shaken even though she immediately discovers his error, she hardly hears him ask her to arrange a rendezvous with another American for him. Later Wilbourne tells several different versions of these events, giving different motives for having asked her the favor. As the novella progresses, the truth behind his statements grows less and less certain. Martha decides at one point that he may even be a chronic liar, incapable of recognizing the truth. What does emerge out of this episode and others like it is that in Martha's world, there are no external certainties. Her loosening grip on reality finally proves so contagious that it infects others. After she describes to George Hartwell her dreams and near-hallucinations, he gets a telephoned request for a meeting from "Gordon Ingram," newly arrived in Rome. He rushes off frantically only to discover *Robert Inman,* an old college classmate. He suffers the explosion of his own emotional depth charge at that point, realizing just how sensitive he has become to Martha's dilemma and just how unsure his own sense of the factual world has become as a result.

The third major difference between the two novellas is the most basic of all: Whereas *The Light in the Piazza* is fundamentally realistic, *Knights and Dragons* has significant allegorical elements. This difference is clearly illustrated by the relationship of each protagonist to the men she meets in Italy. Margaret Johnson's flirtation with Signor Naccarelli is appropriately light and airy. He is admittedly attracted by her: "He could not really say she had made a conquest of him: American women were too confident and brisk; but he could not deny that encounters with her had a certain flavor" (65). She in turn responds to his mature romanticism, and the result, though shy of outright adultery, re-creates in her a sense of her own independent intelligence as well as her mature sexuality. Spencer renders her flirtation with Signor Naccarelli in a traditionally realistic manner; both are fully realized, engagingly comic characters.

In contrast, both Martha's dragon, Gordon Ingram, and her apparent knights, Wilbourne and Hartwell, injure her emotionally while serving as allegorical elements of the novella. "The characters," Spencer has said, "represent elements in a psychic struggle; . . . not all of them and not at every point, but in general. . . . The story becomes a study in evil influences over one woman."[10] The shadowy Gordon Ingram is obviously a demon in Martha's inner world. Even if the reader allows for the subjectivity of her viewpoint, Spencer makes it clear that her former husband dominated and manipulated her. The "evil" in Jim Wilbourne's influence is harder to discover because Martha Ingram is less emotionally involved with him than their physical passion would suggest. However, it is apparent that he uses her physically without ever, so far as the reader knows, committing much time or emotional depth to their relation-

10. Broadwell and Hoag, "Conversation," in *Conversations with Elizabeth Spencer,* ed. Prenshaw, 69.

ship. His apparent inability to tell the truth or even lie consistently rocks her already unstable sense of reality. Even Hartwell, who, as his name suggests, is stability personified, views Martha as the *object* of his chivalry, a wayward damsel whom he may rescue. His first name, George, obviously suggests the myth of St. George and the dragon. But only Martha can save herself, and to do so she must fight off Hartwell's benevolence as well as Ingram's ghost and Wilbourne's indifference. The closing of the novel echoes this governing image of "knights and dragons." Having finally escaped human attachment, Martha Ingram, Spencer emphasizes, "was one of those whom life had held a captive and in freeing herself she had met dissolution" (169). She has paid a desperate price for a desperate freedom.

Spencer's fundamental interest in the ability of these two women to strike a balance between private and communal life is evidence of her continued interest in the dynamics of community. Margaret Johnson rediscovers her sexual and intellectual powers in a new social context, the birthplace of the great European Renaissance. Martha Ingram, crippled by a community of figurative knights and dragons, fights free of their influence into a rarified, acommunal atmosphere in which she responds equally to all people and all environments. By this point in her career, Spencer's characteristic thematic concerns have obviously begun to shape her evolving technical prowess. With *Knights and Dragons,* she first attempts many of the techniques— radical shifts in time, allegorical use of setting and character, highly suggestive imagery—that will characterize much of her later fiction. She developed these techniques as she became increasingly interested in the psychology of her characters, specifically the impact of community on their inner lives.

Coming roughly in the middle of Spencer's career to this point, *The Light in the Piazza* and *Knights and Dragons* illustrate her development clearly. Although she had launched her career as a strict realist, Spencer begins with *Knights and Dragons* to use elements of psychological surrealism. Rather than emphasizing the external development of a traditional plot, as she had in earlier works, she was focusing more on the inner lives of her characters, dramatizing their emotional and psychological development with allegory and imagery. Although *Knights and Dragons* is flawed by the lack of any external correlative to the internal life of Martha Ingram, it foreshadows in technique the larger, more accessible novels that follow.

5 / *A Broken Culture*

He could never understand what they were saying or doing. Who can follow a story any more? What story is worth following? He didn't know.

—*No Place for an Angel*

No Place for an Angel (1967) is one of the major achievements of Elizabeth Spencer's career. Not only a significant work in its own right, it also serves as a milestone in the evolution of her talent. It is the first of a new type of novel for Spencer, intended to dramatize the cultural condition of a large segment of society. Specifically, it addresses the post–World War II nihilism that saturated American society during the 1950s, an entirely new concern for Spencer. Furthermore, it showcases an array of fictional techniques, providing ample evidence that in many ways her abilities had matured to the point that she was able to convey human experience at a new depth and complexity. *No Place for an Angel* is plainly Spencer's most ambitious novel to that point.

Unfortunately, its reception, while often quite respectful, was mixed. Even favorable reviewers, such as Carlos Baker in the *New York Times Book Review,* misread as blind error elements of the novel that Spencer had painstakingly placed there. Baker, for example, condemned the sudden shifts in time and place that Spencer had designed as part of the book's structure. The first edition of the book sold well, but publishers scrapped plans for a paperback edition as objections to the book's apparent lack of structure continued to appear. Despite these contemporary reservations, a retrospective reading reveals that *No Place for an Angel* is a much more highly crafted novel than reviewers originally thought. Spencer succeeds not only in creating suspenseful external action to complement what

Walter Sullivan in his review called her characteristic "introspection," but she does so in a wide range of settings and situations. Reviewers offered universal praise for her style yet failed to notice that she skillfully alternates a variety of styles to reflect the characters or situations in question. Out of this complex of characters, settings, and styles, Spencer intentionally created a *nonstory*, a book whose development is more like that of a symphony than it is like that of a traditional plot. She refuses, in other words, to use a traditional chronology and plot development to portray characters whose lives do not reflect traditional values or traditional communities. Instead, she creates what Melville's Ishmael called a "careful disorderliness," an apparently structureless chaos that reflects the chaos of her characters' lives.[1] For these and other reasons, *No Place for an Angel* is one of Spencer's most successful blendings of theme and technique. Its ambiguity and complexity invite rereading and, more to the point, richly reward it.

No Place for an Angel is the first example of the new type of novel Spencer began to write in the 1960s. Whereas before she had always set the action of her books within the context of a small community, in *No Place for an Angel* she addressed communal issues as they affected life across a wide cultural context. After setting two novellas in Italy, she began to write novels she intended as comments on American culture, a curious blend of social and psychological fiction. In *No Place for an Angel*, Spencer takes on no less a subject than the rootless, power-drunk culture that fighting and winning World War II created in America. As a central character, Irene Waddell, realizes, "She . . . like all her generation . . . [had] been created by the war."[2] She sees the postwar years as both "delicate and brutal"; one must act with great delicacy simply to avoid the meanness bred into the American spirit by the war (185). One by one the characters of *No Place for an Angel* realize the deeply rooted nihilism that pervades their culture. They are political and social experts in an age when mass-media politics and fashionable society have replaced traditional

1. Carlos Baker, "Two American Marriages," *New York Times Book Review,* October 22, 1967, p. 8; Walter Sullivan, "Fiction in a Dry Season: Some Signs of Hope," *Sewanee Review,* LXXVII (Winter, 1969), 163; Herman Melville, *Moby-Dick* (Boston, 1956), 283.

2. Elizabeth Spencer, *No Place for an Angel* (New York, 1967), 22. Hereinafter cited by page number in the text.

community. As a result, they all experience an existential loneliness and frustration despite their well-publicized successes.

No Place for an Angel represents perhaps Spencer's greatest achievement in creating a complex of characters from which no individual stands out. The cast of the novel is so closely intertwined that even in a section focusing on an individual or couple, the other characters are constantly present in what they think and say. The cast of *No Place for an Angel* is unique among those of Spencer's novels because they are, with only one exception, both wealthy and famous. Catherine's husband, Jerry Sasser, has appeared on the cover of a national news magazine as one of Washington's most powerful young political operatives. When Irene and Charles Waddell sailed from Europe, they and their children "were photographed on the first class deck, and their picture appeared in the Paris *Herald Tribune,* the Rome *Daily American* and one of the Italian papers" (245–46). Several years after her affair with Mario Marcadante, Irene "was to see pictures of this man and his lovely wife in an international fashion magazine. It was a full spread, showing their villa at Fregene, their three children, their graceful little boat, and the signora herself in several of the latest Roman fashions created for women like herself" (227). They are newsstand people, a web of internationally sophisticated power brokers whose personal lives are almost completely subsumed by political and material ambitions. Spencer uses them, the best and brightest of their generation, to satirize the failure of that generation.

As a way of emphasizing the emptiness of their culture, Spencer makes each of the characters of *No Place for an Angel* exceptionally gifted. Charles Waddell is an international businessman whose arrogance and lack of tact dated from the war and grew as he "painfully learned that warmth and affection were generally misunderstood, all too often taken advantage of, and were the American mannerism Europeans were quickest to view with contempt" (245). His genius lies in quick, decisive action, the independent manipulation of power, and, ironically, in following the social lead of his wife. Irene is a well-known socialite; she has an astonishing sense of fashion, knowing instinctively which clothes, styles, perfumes, and functions are seasonally powerful. "Practically everybody in the world is out of it," she believes. "I will always be in it. . . . I created it. It is me" (269). Her social expertise supports her husband's career, and his income makes that expertise possible. The Waddells are quintessential American power brokers who combine business and social acumen.

However, even the Waddells' power is eclipsed by that of Jerry Sasser when backed by his wife Catherine's money. A veteran who returns from the war stripped of all idealism, he cold-bloodedly pursues the glory of Washington politics as an aide to a prominent senator. "Politics, tension, women" make up the element in which he swims (73), and his genius, as his wife knows only too well, is in manipulating others. "He has a talent," she tells her sister, "for getting people to feel the way he wants them to feel. Not just say they feel that way, but really feel that way" (93). Sensitive to the moral emptiness of his world, Catherine develops as her great talent the ability for withdrawal. "Catherine was leaving them inexorably again," Barry Day realizes at one point, and "was by now no more than a speck disappearing at high speed into distant light" (58). Thinking of Catherine, Irene "perceived a clear spirit groping out of the dark" (239), an apt image for Catherine's desire to escape the postwar world.

The one character of significance who lacks all prominence, wealth, or influence is the sculptor Barry Day. His great talent is for seeing: "Surfaces drew him as if many magnets had been secretly installed in them. . . . Door sills, the full firm limbs of girls, their knees, ankles, etc., babies' heels and eyebrows, the slippery hexagonal surface of a beer stein, the flat composed length of the bar, a man's shoulder beneath an unpressed coat . . . anything he clapped eyes on he seemed to stick to" (15).

Barry's talent, like Catherine's, is plainly unmarketable; he discovers neither inspiration nor audience in postwar America. By populating the novel primarily with people of wealth, influence, and ability, Spencer emphasizes that even they find happiness impossible in the world they have created. She dramatizes this, characteristically, by stressing the abject failure of any relationship between them. Though all are socially adept, their ability goes only cocktail-party deep. Their marriages are corrupt, their love affairs doomed, and even their simplest friendships suspect.

Of the two central marriages in the book, one is successful on the surface, but neither is a true emotional union. Jerry and Catherine Sasser have known each other from childhood but lost all sense of intimate companionship during the war. He is so changed by military service that Catherine tells her sister, only half in jest, that perhaps an uncaring imposter killed him and took his place while he was overseas. By the time Jerry has risen to the height of his political influence and they might most enjoy their marriage, his infidelities are legion, and Catherine is being driven insane by his lack of concern. He is willing to see her hospitalized for counseling but whisks her back to Washington immediately when he needs her to appear as a hostess. She leaves him after he tries to use her family's money to buy his way out of a political misplay. Disgusted, he later takes advantage of her emotional confusion to accuse her of trying to kill him. Much like Martha Ingram in *Knights and Dragons,* she eventually finds limited happiness living a quiet, relatively isolated life. Sasser himself drifts into the obscurity of the "grey world" he lives in, the victim of his own political nihilism.

The Waddells' marriage, on the other hand, appears successful, but Spencer's close scrutiny reveals not only the emotional void between them but also the way in which they bring out the worst in each other. When Charles realizes that Irene has taken an Italian lover, he only bides his time, counting on her materialism to bring her back to him. Later, when they are reunited, Catherine asks them to help Barry Day recover some sculpture he left in Italy. They refuse matter-of-factly. After Catherine leaves, Irene "laughed. 'I guess she thought we cared' " (247). Their marriage is at best a cult of cold-blooded competence from which they cast sarcastic judgment on those around them. They thrive on each other's acquisitive strengths. Whereas Catherine fails to divorce Jerry Sasser out of emotional inertia, Irene refuses to leave Charles Waddell for her lover because of the financial security Charles represents.

Even the one couple whose kindness and gentleness with each other link them throughout the book fail to form a lasting bond. After leaving her husband, Catherine Sasser meets Barry Day in Italy, and they take up visiting the beach and sightseeing together. Only once do they meet as lovers, some years later in New York. This spark of passion is ignited by Catherine's imminent meeting with her husband; even Barry realizes that she slept with him to steel herself for "something far nearer to the quick of her than he could ever get" (55). In this nihilistic world where images of jet liners have replaced those of angels, active, aggressive people care more for power than for each other, and passive characters like Barry and Catherine are all but helpless.

When intense relationships do flourish for a time, they do so in an isolated spot, often in the presence, real or imagined, of a third party. Barry and Catherine's moment of physical passion—she recalled "his eagerness to please, hold, stabilize, satisfy her" (267)—occurs only once and then in the context of Catherine's fear of her husband. Irene Waddell's idyllic affair with Mario occurs in the isolated coastal city of Siracusa, where she has gone to rescue a gravely ill Barry Day. As Barry recovers from infection, he "came alive out of himself slowly but unmistakenly to the distantly perceived rhythm of Irene and Mario, somewhere together." But "he never criticized. They had a fine abundance he would not like to be caught quarreling with; by having him as an excuse they just missed the awful expertness they might have had if it had all been done on purpose. They owe it all to me, damn them, he thought" (212). This passage describing the strange dreamy threesome that the lovers and Day together make far from Rome recalls the family "circle" of three described by Arney Talliafero in *This Crooked Way*. In both instances all three individuals are nourished, even inspired in some obscure way.

As ill as he is, Barry Day dreams of the interlude lasting: "Now a real change had come about: to Barry it was more profound than the inevitable fact that Irene and Mario had become lovers. It had happened to all of them, the three of them, and he was as much a part of it as they. It had happened while the two of them made love and while he lay mending, watching their faces when he could and when he couldn't watching the curtains, the sun, the shore and the sea. Siracusa. It was a refuge. . . . It felt like home" (214).

Siracusa provides the three a still point in a spinning world, but the world, in the form of Irene's husband, invades and destroys it. Barry is disoriented, Mario distraught, but Irene, despite her physical infatuation, is almost relieved. She realizes intuitively part of Spencer's message, that loving affection cannot survive in her world. The angel of the title is not an individual but an ideal—self-sacrificing love shared on a consistent, daily basis between people. It is the angel of communion.[3]

*   *   *

3. The one exception to the rule of miscommunication and disunion in the novel is the Waddells' twin sons. By some mysterious genetic power they think and act in perfect synchronization and are impervious to unhappiness. Their intelligence and ability comfort both their parents, but Spencer hints that even their harmony cannot survive adulthood.

In portraying this dishearteningly "grey world," Spencer calls on a larger array of techniques than any she has used before. She intentionally interweaves scenes from a wide variety of times and places, a feature contemporary reviewers often misread as sloppy design or editing. In addition, she often shifts the center of her limited omniscience from character to character as she moves backward and forward in time. While doing so, she varies her style to complement the character or group she is portraying, revealing for the first time a fluent flexibility in style. The novel is not divided into traditional chapters, which might have made all these transitions easier to follow, but rather long sections much like the movements in a symphony. This nontraditional structure serves to focus the reader's attention on what Spencer called "the crossings of many people's paths" rather than the people themselves.[4] Finally, she addresses all the denizens of her "grey world" with an ironic tone that reveals through their words and deeds their overly inflated views of themselves.

Early in the novel, Spencer uses Barry Day's confusion over the intricacies of the plots of *Perry Mason* television shows to hint at her own motives in designing the book as she does. Watching television in a bar, Barry is drawn to a show that the narrator says will be "about people. . . . It will not tell any one story, for there is no story." The other patrons suddenly demand that the channel be changed to *Perry Mason,* the ultimate in suspenseful drama. But poor Barry "could never understand what [the characters on the detective show] were saying or doing. Who can follow a story any more? What story is worth following? He didn't know" (14–15). That there is "no story" in *No Place for an Angel* is precisely the point; in a world gone mad not even Perry Mason (whose first name echoes Barry's) can unravel a traditional plot and discover the culprit.

The most disturbing of Spencer's "no story" techniques to her contemporaries was apparently her radical shifts in time and place. Spencer herself provided the best clue to understanding the novel's buried structure in her 1975 interview with Charles Bunting: "I think in any work you must have a sort of feeling of unity and euphony. There's a musical texture that any work will set up, whether it's a work of three pages or three hundred pages, . . . so the

4. Broadwell and Hoag, "Conversation," in *Conversations with Elizabeth Spencer,* ed. Prenshaw, 71.

flow in a way is musical in a novel. To me a novel is like a symphony in many respects."[5]

This analogy suggests a clear pattern to the apparently scrambled events of *No Place for an Angel*. Spencer's comparison of a novel with a symphony suggests in turn that this novel's four sections—"Blood Sports," "Dangerous Journeys," "Where Paths Divide," and "The Grey World"—should be read as a symphony's four movements. In the first movement, a fifty-eight-page section entitled "Blood Sports," present time is 1958, and the action moves from June more or less straightforwardly through the summer and fall, with Spencer dropping the traditional clues as to passage of time and location of action. While the action centers around the Waddells and Barry Day, Catherine Sasser appears, and there are a number of references to Mario, the Italian city Siracusa, and a mysterious past in general. At the end of the section, Barry tells the Waddells that Catherine has suddenly disappeared again, as is her habit. He says that hers is a "dangerous journey," adding "I guess all journeys are dangerous" (57). Spencer thus establishes the motif of the long second movement (188 pages), which is entitled "Dangerous Journeys."

In the first part of this movement, Spencer centers the point of view in Catherine Sasser, who flies out of New York five pages into the section. There, the flashes backward and forward in time begin. Having eased her readers into the texture of these lives, Spencer suddenly takes them spinning off on another plane flight from years before, when the Sassers traveled together toward a desperate separation, and from there further and further back in time to Jerry Sasser and Catherine Latham's shared childhood in Merrill, Texas. It becomes obvious that these journeys are dangerous because they are primarily inner ones.[6] "Dangerous Journeys" contains four numbered sections: the first is centered primarily in Catherine Sasser; the second primarily in Irene Waddell (recalling her affair with Mario in Siracusa); the third primarily in Barry Day (recalling his meeting Catherine in Italy); and the fourth shifting about to gather the various

5. Charles T. Bunting, " 'In That Time and at That Place': The Literary World of Elizabeth Spencer," in *Conversations with Elizabeth Spencer,* ed. Prenshaw, 28.

6. There is a sense in which several of the "dangerous" journeys of the second movement might be described as Freudian. They usually involve searching through past events for clues to the present personalities of characters. In the case of Jerry and Catherine Sasser, Spencer's emphasis on their childhoods certainly suggests a Freudian reading.

narrative threads. "As in Perry Mason, the gun was there and the man looked dead. You could figure it out any way you wanted to" (249).

The final two movements in the novel continue the pattern established in "Dangerous Journeys," shifting from character to character, moving the reader even more freely through time and space. "Where Paths Divide" emphasizes the slowly growing divisions between these persons whose lives had for years been intertwined. "The Grey World," though it offers no courtroom climaxes or resolutions, shows how these lives wind down toward atrophy. The characters increasingly sense the "greyness" of their world with its lack of moral distinctions. Their lives have degenerated into loneliness and failure—or at best the shabby, second-rate success of the Waddells. In its symphonic structure, *No Place for an Angel* is a book of artful disorder, stressing the emotional chaos and failures of its characters' lives by re-creating in the way it is told their lack of direction.

Although the original reviewers of *No Place for an Angel* recognized immediately this lack of continuity in time and space, they did not seem to notice the complementary shifts in style. Granville Hicks praised Spencer's language because it "ranges easily from the calmly factual to the beautifully evocative," but he did so apparently without realizing that Spencer alters her style radically to fit the characters involved. Prenshaw was the first to comment on Spencer's use of a wide range of styles but without recognizing that these shifts are fundamental to both the structural message and the psychological portraiture of the novel. Spencer herself made it clear as early as 1975 that she does not "write in any one style." She remarked in an interview: "The style that I can express myself best in any one story or one novel bends itself flexibly to the situation, characters, and moments of the story. . . . And this extends . . . to the realm of the sentences themselves. . . . One character may take over whose style of speaking and thinking is at variance with the general tone of the book, but always it's different in a counterpointing sense, so that you're varying from the prevailing style in order to return to it."[7] This "counterpointing" is an integral part of the musical structure of *No Place for an Angel*, one of the chief clues that the novel's disorderliness is carefully orchestrated.

7. Granville Hicks, "Lives Like Assorted Pastries," *Saturday Review,* October 21, 1967, p. 29; Prenshaw, *Elizabeth Spencer,* 102; Bunting, " 'In That Time,' " in *Conversations with Elizabeth Spencer,* ed. Prenshaw, 28.

Each of the five central characters in the novel is associated with a distinct style that Spencer uses to counterpoint the narrator's generally ironic tone. As Prenshaw notes, the language of Jerry Sasser's sections is "a kind of exaggerated, haunted prose consisting of figurative language, flashbacks, memories recollected through a collage of images, and hallucinations or fantasies," all of which "reveals the desperate emptiness of his life." The style associated with his wife, Catherine, is also deeply reflective but even more divorced from the present-tense corporeal world, much more slowly paced, less dense and desperate. Catherine's thoughts always carry a tone of longing, even of sentimentality. Because Charles Waddell is totally self-obsessed, the style Spencer uses in portraying him centers on first-person pronouns and consists almost totally of his opinions and others' reactions to them. With the exception of the dreamy interlude at Siracusa, Irene Waddell's sections are full of the details of fashionable society, written with the cutting irony of "a novel of manners."[8] The style of Barry Day's passages is the most concrete, the most sensuous of all. To reflect his artist's sensibility, Spencer writes an almost primitive language of the senses, a world where "two glasses . . . on the dusty table [and] . . . cigarettes . . . left to smoke themselves down to ash" represent the climax of his affair with Catherine (56). Expanding on the techniques she developed in *Knights and Dragons,* Spencer uses prose style to draw psychological portraits, once again taking a stylistic gamble to force her reader deeper inside her characters.

To stress that the overall sense of chaos in the novel is a function of her characters' lives, Spencer adopts a consistently ironic tone as a background to the stylistic motifs of her various characters. She takes none of these characters as seriously as they take themselves, and she reveals as much in what she has them do and say. The novel opens with the artist Barry Day proclaiming to Irene Waddell that he intends to carve an angel as the ultimate expression of his sensibility; her casual remark that "angels don't belong in America" deflates his fragile ego and sets the tone for what is to follow (3). Spencer is careful to point out that though each character has genius, genius is not enough in this amoral world. Each character fails notably in the very medium to which he or she is dedicated. Barry Day never carves an angel; he ends by taking on the quintessential middle-class

8. Prenshaw, *Elizabeth Spencer,* 102, 101.

life, giving up all his artistic pretension for life in the suburbs. Jerry Sasser fails to cover his senator's tracks on a sensitive equal-rights issue and, despite his charisma, fades into political obscurity. Ironically, his own arrogance and misjudgment prove his undoing. His long-suffering wife, Catherine, whose gift had been "to love, to love, to love, constantly, the very rhythm of it like a beating heart" (270), cannot bear the brunt of the world's brutality and so lives a solitary life. Ideally suited for communal sharing, she fails at both marriage and friendship. Charles Waddell's brash self-assurance had led to wartime success both in the army and in international business. In the 1950s, however, his self-assurance becomes arrogance: "The complaint was, verbatim: He can't take his army boots off" (19). He survives in less affluent, less lucrative positions primarily through the social savvy of his wife. Like the others, he dies on the sword by which he has lived—the ultimate irony for a generation bred on conflict.

Of the main characters, only Irene Waddell seems to succeed in her field of expertise, but Spencer takes care to reveal just how hollow are her victories. Near the end of the novel she sits perfectly attired in her Manhattan apartment as the maid prepares for a dinner party. Troubled by a visit from Catherine Sasser, her thoughts drift: "And all over the city, swarming, the unknown, the voiceless, the quiet, the good, the evil, the loud, the corrupt, the sick, the dying, millions on millions, reached out to one another, caught and held or failed to catch and hold. To be good, not to be mad, to accept, live, perceive, with steadfastness and grace . . . was that all? To love, to love, to love, constantly, the very rhythm of it like a beating heart? What about it chilled her, touched her with dread? She lit a cigarette and stubbed it out" (270–71).

She is haunted by a vague sense of guilt even though she is unable to conceive of action based on anything so simpleminded as goodness or love. She snaps out of her reverie, however, when she notices the maid's misplacement of the flowers. " 'Not there,' she said. . . . 'You can't put red chrysanthemums next to goldfish. Put them on the other side of the room' " (271). Irene Waddell's social genius, as powerful as it is, is spiritually barren. Spencer's ironic tone makes it clear that all of these characters, even Catherine Sasser, are spiritual invalids. There is no context in which "to be good, not to be mad," is enough for these lost souls. They have all cut their ties to any community, which in Spencer's world is the source of spirituality.

As a result, they drift constantly, both literally across the globe and figuratively within themselves.

Spencer's comments in a number of interviews suggest that she believes spiritual health comes from one of two sources—place or community. Read in a body, her fiction reinforces this idea. In *No Place for an Angel* Catherine Sasser's childhood farm and the seaside city of Siracusa in Italy take on mystical properties. Each has a spirit to which Catherine on one hand and Irene and Barry on the other respond. They are unable to maintain their proper relationships to these places, however, and so lose the love and affection they know there. The other spiritual haven available to Spencer's characters is that of true community. Catherine's tie to her two old, unmarried uncles and Irene's circle of love that encompasses Mario Marcadante and Barry Day are both communities that nourish and define their members. Catherine's slowly unfolding, largely celibate relationship with Barry Day is another example of an intimacy that, for a time at least, provides peace and security: "They were giving each other health, that precious thing so few people will think they ever need" (231). Despite the deeply rooted longing for permanence on the part of those involved in all these communities, they are far too fragile to last in the world of jet-fueled international politics. These characters are profoundly rootless; they have "all been just about everywhere" and so can maintain no vital connection to any place or anyone (269).

No marriage, affair, or friendship of any depth survives in the novel. The Waddells' social expertise masks an almost total lack of intimacy; their secret reaction to those they entertain so expertly is world-weariness and sarcasm. Spencer has created a cast of characters who have traded away spiritual communion for power and prestige. The result is a world that cripples even those, like Catherine, who would return to simpler times. Spencer's tone in response can only be ironic, even in places satiric. The angel for whom there is no place is the angel of communion, that mystical connection to place or to another that Spencer holds most sacred. In the absence of that angel, Spencer's is a delicately vicious "grey world," where individuals, no matter how brilliant, die from the inside out.

Spencer designed the carefully constructed disorder in the novel to convey the lack of direction, the spiritual drift of disconnected lives. Near the end of the novel, Jerry Sasser realizes: "No, in spite of all the shaking and worrying he had taken care to give it, life was not even a story. It all pranced away like a mad chorus line" (301–302). Read in the context of her earlier studies of community, *No Place for an Angel* provides a clear portrait of what happens when individuals are stripped of nurturing community. Their lives cease to make narrative as well as emotional sense, and the result is *No Place for an Angel*, an artfully composed symphony that ends on an intentionally frustrating note of discordant laughter.

If, as Spencer suggests, her novels are like symphonies, *No Place for an Angel* has fallen on increasingly deaf ears. Ironically, it is the first of her mature novels—large in scope, ambitious in theme, and sophisticated in technique. Like *The Snare* and *The Salt Line*, which follow, *No Place for an Angel* requires more of its readers than the traditionally structured *Voice at the Back Door*. It is also similar to the novels that follow in that it rewards successive readings by opening up a larger, more complex world of character and situation. Leaving the family and community-bound environs of Mississippi must have proved difficult for Spencer as an artist, but the move paid off in works both increasingly sophisticated and increasingly rich.

6 / Life's Snare

Following the ambitious *No Place for an Angel*, Elizabeth Spencer published in 1972 what remains to this day both her best and most underrated novel. *The Snare* follows the pattern Spencer established with *No Place for an Angel* by addressing "not the Southern world, but the world of modern experience." Although it is set in a prominent southern city, New Orleans, *The Snare* is not, as Randy Woodland points out, "a New Orleans novel. . . . It is clear that at the center of the novel is not the actual place New Orleans, but the *idea* of New Orleans." Spencer uses her abstracted New Orleans, she has said, to "illuminate an area of modern experience that has to do with the underground."[1] By *underground* Spencer refers to the seamy underside of New Orleans life that holds a powerful attraction for her protagonist, Julia Garrett. Drugs, murder, rape, a stolen and then lost body, torture, voodoo, impetuous sexuality—all interwoven against a background of Bourbon Street jazz. This "crooked world," as Spencer calls it in the novel, is more real to Julia Garrett than her affluent life in Audubon Place, an old-money enclave of New Orleans wealth and power. Spencer has said that she uses this situation to investigate the growth of a counterculture in postwar America, but *The Snare* is more a moral than a sociological tale: The

1. Bunting, " 'In That Time,' " in *Conversations with Elizabeth Spencer*, ed. Prenshaw, 32; Randy Woodland, " 'In That City Foreign and Paradoxical': The Idea of New Orleans in the Southern Literary Imagination" (Ph.D. dissertation, University of North Carolina, 1987), 299 (emphasis mine).

force that compels Julia Garrett is much the same force that drives Young Goodman Brown into the midnight forest two centuries before. The primary difference between the two is that Julia Garrett is strong enough to withstand the consequences.

Her emotional resilience is the culmination of what was for Spencer a serious artistic quest. In 1982 she told Elizabeth Broadwell and Ronald Hoag that beginning with Margaret Johnson of *The Light in the Piazza* she had searched for a woman character "who could sustain a weight of experience, both intellectual and emotional." The search was unsuccessful for a time. "But when I finally discovered Julia," Spencer recalled, "I found in her a person who could take it and survive."[2]

What Julia has to "take and survive" is a world that contains many of the same ingredients as a *film noir* murder mystery. *The Snare*, however, is a murder mystery Spencer style, in which the ultimate clue to the communal horror is the horror within Julia Garrett and the ultimate solution lies buried within her complex personality. Julia, like the imagined New Orleans that Spencer creates around her, is dark, sensuous, and sexy. Spencer has said bluntly that her "New Orleans is a very sexy place" and that she needed "a very sexy heroine to make that connection plain." The design of the novel emphasizes the connection between its heroine and its setting so strongly because Spencer intended them to reflect each other, Julia Garrett acting as a "human compendium of the city" and the plot as it unfolds there. "New Orleans," according to Spencer, "reveals the woman and the woman reveals New Orleans."[3]

If *The Snare* is a modernist murder mystery, there are at least four significant clues to its solution. Although there is a fascinating unsolved murder at the core of the external plot, the novel's real mystery is the nature of the city and of Julia. The first clue to the puzzle lies in the complex external-internal juxtaposition of Spencer's New Orleans with Julia Garrett's spiritual and emotional life. The second has to do with the nature of the two worlds that Julia finds superimposed one upon the other—the "straight world" of normal existence and the "crooked world" of New Orleans' darker side. Through her cyclical relations with the men who are drawn to

2. Broadwell and Hoag, "Conversation," in *Conversations with Elizabeth Spencer*, ed. Prenshaw, 75.

3. Roberts, "Whole Personality," in *Conversations with Elizabeth Spencer*, ed. Prenshaw, 228.

her, Julia penetrates deeper and deeper into the best and worst of her own nature as well as that of the city. These relationships constitute Spencer's third important clue. What Julia discovers in them about communion constitutes the fourth. For at its deepest level, *The Snare* returns to what has long been Spencer's central concern, the nature of the communal bond between group and individual.

The demands of that theme had created for Spencer a complex of technical questions at least as early as the writing of *Knights and Dragons*. How does one portray the effect of community relations on the internal life of an individual? How portray the complex way in which a communal group reflects the psychology of its members? How can a writer fully explore the desires and needs of complex individuals as they externalize themselves in the context of community? How, in other words, can she do artistic justice to the external as well as the internal lives of her characters simultaneously? Spencer's juxtaposition of Julia Garrett with New Orleans is her strongest reply to date. As a result, *The Snare* is at once her most complex and her most rewarding novel.

All of the novel's primary characters are aware of the city's "dark world," its mysterious "second life webbed invisibly in with their own."[4] Those who know Julia Garrett intimately also associate her with the dark life of the city. Martin Parham, scion of a wealthy Mississippi family and an early lover of Julia's, "had said that to him she was the whole city; . . . its life was hers and hers its own" (162). The itinerant Jake Springland, who drifts into New Orleans in search of jazz, both musical and human, also becomes Julia's lover, a "crooked" counterpoint to the "straight" Martin Parham. Springland, like Parham, sought in Julia "the city's rough corruption with its core of feeling, its peculiar tolerant knowledge" (117–18). Unlike Parham, Springland took Julia herself closer to the "knowledge" that they both sought: "She gave to him to get in return what he had found there," the lifeblood of the city (118). Even Tommy Arnold, who for years had chased the secret essence of New Orleans as a crime reporter, found in Julia "the ways of the dark world that lay all around them" (81–82).

Spencer's New Orleans, like her protagonist, is a complex blend

4. Elizabeth Spencer, *The Snare* (New York, 1972), 81. Hereinafter cited by page number in the text.

of cultural influences and socioeconomic layers. Through Julia Garrett's Uncle Maurice and Aunt Isabel Devigny, she provides a detailed picture of life in prestigious Audubon Place, an exclusive neighborhood off St. Charles Avenue. The couple's Old World charm and influential social connections belie a physical as well as emotional sterility. Their utter devotion to each other within their sheltered life is touching but ultimately quite fragile. They and their circle have neither the emotional toughness nor the willing intensity that Julia seeks from early in life. Maurice's father, Henri Devigny—who may have abused Julia sexually—opens up to her and by extension the reader an older New Orleans of quadroon mistresses and partisan politics. "Webbed" into the social fabric of the Devignys' straight New Orleans is a nighttime world of crime and jazz, sexuality and violence. Due partly to the influence of her Great Uncle Dev, Julia realizes early that the city draws the intensity and rhythms of its life from the corruption at its core.

Like Dev, her guardian mentor, and in many ways like the city itself, Julia can find emotional release only in the underworld of her life. This "dark of the moon" (372)—the jazz and drugs, petty theft and seedy apartments—is attractive to her partly because it is "not subject to approval by the proper side of New Orleans, of which her family was a part."[5] Julia is torn between the security and peace of Audubon Place, with its projected marriage to Martin Parham, and the dangerous struggle of life on the edge of an abyss. Despite her social advantages and electric sexuality, Julia is often lonely, "singular to the point of being waif like" with "no society in the world of other women" (140). Her motives are often as much a mystery to herself as to those around her. She almost never acts "with calculation" (235) and is as independent, Spencer notes time and again, as a cat.

What drives her from early in the novel is the restless sense that there is more to life than the staid, self-righteous existence of her aunt and uncle. Her early and intense exposure to the dark French Dev creates and nurses within her the need to join the intensity of illicitness with the peace of a secure life. "In search of synthesis," as Spencer puts it, "she went deeper and deeper into seedy, cruel, even criminal life."[6] After nearly destroying herself, what she discovers is: "Life is

5. Roberts, "Whole Personality," in *Conversations with Elizabeth Spencer*, ed. Prenshaw, 228.
6. *Ibid.*

a tree with twin trunks, one is love and the other corruption—if she had settled for anything weaker than that, life would never forgive her" (388). She realizes that "people draw life from the crooked world" in order to love and be loved (110). The violence and pain that Julia discovers at the core of the city are in several respects the culmination of a motif in Spencer's work that was present as early as the aptly named *This Crooked Way*, with its voodoo curses and gris-gris packets. The underworld surfaces again in *The Voice at the Back Door* in the form of the mobsters who accidentally shoot Jimmy Tallant. *No Place for an Angel* takes as a central premise that political and social corruption had saturated postwar America. It is in *The Snare*, however, that Spencer first investigates the underworld's hypnotic attraction for all the intense, restless characters of her fictional world. As Julia Garrett becomes increasingly aware of the intimate bond between herself and the city she loves, she realizes that it is the "conversation going on" between the straight and crooked worlds that "makes [the] city and . . . makes the world" (110).

One reason she is so sensitive to this mysterious dialogue is the advantages that the straight world has offered her. Orphaned in early childhood, she was adopted by the Devignys and brought to live in the plush mansion at Audubon Place. She has all the advantages of a well-established, upper-class life, seeming even to fill the void of Maurice and Isabel's childlessness. She is engaged for a time to Martin Parham, whose family, according to Tommy Arnold, owns "half the state" of Mississippi (111). She has, in other words, the opportunity to join wealth to status and live a debutante's happily-ever-after. She cuts Parham and his money loose, however, and in trying to explain why to others, she begins to understand herself. She hates the money hunger and empty affection, the "time sequence and filing systems" (240), the self-righteousness and emotional hypocrisy of the safe but shallow life. "I want the depth," she tells Tommy Arnold. "I have to have it, and when I get it, then I'm with it, with life, you know" (112).

When her common-law relationship with Jake Springland begins to settle into too predictable a pattern and they begin to behave like a careful, mature couple, she realizes they have lost their mutual magic: "What she called it to herself was the Charade. A Charade in human relationships is a mask over what is really going on" (145). She realizes eventually that nearly all social relationships are charades, intended to protect individuals from one another and from themselves. Increasingly she seeks in those around her a deeper level of honesty, no matter how painful. Ironically, this means that she must turn, even in her relations with Martin Parham, to what she calls the crooked world.

She lives for a period of time as Martin's mistress in a house that he has bought for her maintenance. Although he has married and become a father since she broke their engagement, he dreams aloud of leaving his wife for her. She blithely sidesteps his offers and the conventional morality they imply, pointing out that marriage would ruin their relationship. In accepting Parham but not his offers of marriage, she protects her sense of "a purity of intention in herself" (147). She realizes in time that there is a "self within herself" that is attracted to fear, even violence (273), a crookedness that she suspects is "webbed invisibly in" everyone around her (81). She ceases to trust those who bank on the security of the straight world, those who deny any moral doubt or flaw in themselves.

She turns instead to Jake Springland a second time and to the dangerous characters with whom he is linked. She seeks there a depth, a passion, a "purity of intent" both in them and in herself. What she discovers is horror. She and Springland are kidnapped, fed drugs, and forced to commit humiliating sex acts. At the lowest point, however, it is not physical pain or emotional humiliation that touches her, but the realization that "there's nothing [she] couldn't do," that there had been "something in [her] that wanted . . . the worst that could happen" (343). From this depth she envisions life as a tree with the twin trunks of love and corruption (388). She realizes at this point the full import of what she had intuited, that communion with others depends on accepting both the purity *and* the corruption within. At the end of the novel, "All [New Orleans] to Julia was like a jewel—real or fake, what did it matter? It spangled around [her] in eternal light, silently rejoicing" (406). What she has discovered is that the city, like her, is simultaneously real and fake, crooked as well as straight.

With the exception of Julia's Aunt Isabel, the other significant characters in the novel are men, all of whom are intensely involved with Julia, all of whom except her uncle become her lovers.[7] Her

---

7. It is impossible to be sure from the text whether Julia's mentor, Henri Devigny, actually seduces her as child; her memory of the event, though sexually charged, is too vague. It is also not clear whether during the long night of torture she is raped by Ted Marnie, her kidnapper. Spencer does suggest, however, that in each instance a violation occurred, one loving and one hateful.

cyclical relations with these men form the structure of Spencer's narrative, reflecting Julia's growing understanding of her own nature and that of the city. Martin Parham, to whom Julia is engaged prior to the opening of the novel, represents the quintessentially straight life. Once his infatuation with Julia became obvious, all who knew them predicted marriage, unable to conceive of a woman rejecting the Parham wealth. "Even Cadillacs get dull" (111), however, and Julia breaks their engagement in search of "depth." She discovers it in the form of Jake Springland, Korean War veteran, jazz noviate, and drifter. When the novel opens, Springland has been jailed on a murder charge, which only intensifies Julia's interest in him. After he is acquitted, they move in together, seeking an open, spontaneous, passionate relationship. Partly as a result of Jake's artistic failure, their relationship slips into the false affectations of a charade, and they part.

In the long central section of the novel entitled "The In-Between Time," Julia drifts back into contact with the now-married Martin Parham and becomes his mistress. His insensitivity to the full range of her emotional life leads to a second break-up, and suddenly men she had thought lost to her begin to reappear. The deranged charlatan Ted Marnie, whom Jake Springland had been accused of murdering, suddenly resurfaces in California. Springland is brought back to New Orleans by the police, and a new cycle of relationships begins. Even though Springland had married during "the in-between time," Julia moves back in with him after his second release by the police. She becomes pregnant, just before the two are kidnapped and brutalized by Marnie. She survives to bear her child, Emile, and finally settles into a relatively stable life with Tommy Arnold, the reporter with whom Spencer opened the novel over four hundred pages before.

Arnold is, like Julia, suspended between the straight and crooked worlds. Of all those who touch her deeply, he comes the closest to balancing the need for security and affection with the need for intensity and release. Spencer suspends four other significant figures around them like points on a moral compass. To one side, in the crooked world of spontaneity and instinct, looms the figure of Jake Springland. Opposite, caught in the straightlaced, profit-motivated straight world, is Martin Parham. Neither direction alone orients a full human being. After the slow recovery of her wits following her kidnapping and the birth of Emile, Julia describes for Tommy Arnold the other two reference points in her private universe. Having seen

Marnie's corpse in the bottom of a well, she remains haunted by the Dantesque image of her torturer.

When I close my eyes to sleep, to nap, to rest them, even to blink, I see that face. Sometimes I see Dev's face too, in clouds, dark and thundery or looking out of high windows . . . always looking down at me, about to say my name. He up high and Ted Marnie down low. . . . Christ, Tommy, can you think how it is? I mean for everybody there's a place where the thinking runs out and the world's held in place by something that's not known about really, a mystery, some people say God. For me, there's what I'm telling you. There are these two. (401)

Above her hangs her mysterious Great Uncle Dev, who taught her the desire and the strength to see the world whole. Below her is frozen her personal Satan, the "soul engineer" Marnie, who taught her the extent of her own moral culpability. Three of the four—Dev, Parham, Marnie—are dead by the end of the novel, and the fourth—Springland—gone for good. And yet, she has internalized them all and, through them, a profound vision of herself and her city.

Spencer uses these cycles of love and sexuality to structure *The Snare*, dramatizing through Julia's relations with men her growing understanding of her world. She is the detective who leads the reader deeper and deeper into her city while searching for clues to her own psychic identity. During the novel's long first part, she discovers through her affair with Springland the extent of the underworld that is "webbed" throughout New Orleans. At the same time, she realizes fully her own inability to live a straight life and the degree to which she is fulfilled by the underworld. During "The In-Between Time," her stint as Martin Parham's "fancy woman" reminds her of her deeply rooted desire for children and a safe environment in which to raise them. When Springland returns to her life, his attraction for her is as intense as ever, but she wants more from him now—stability and commitment as well as passion and spontaneity. His acceptance for a time as a member of one of New Orleans' best Dixieland bands introduces her to communion among equals as the ultimate answer to her search. Her debasement at the hands of Marnie is the final cycle in her quest, the final clue to the solution of her mystery. *Her* life, she realizes, like the life of her city, "is a tree with twin trunks . . . love and . . . corruption" (388). Neither can exist without the other; deny either and death is the result.

For the reader the most disturbing scene in this quest is probably not the night of drug-induced debauchery. Spencer treats that in retrospect from the morning after, when both Springland and Julia struggle to recover their emotional equilibrium. Although Spencer obviously intends her readers to sense fully the intimate horror of that night, the scene in Jackson Park from the previous day is in many ways more unsettling. There, on a public park bench, Julia tells Jake that she is pregnant, realizing even as she tells him that he is slipping away from her: "She was mewing about already in abandonment, a deserted pet unable to leave the house everyone had moved from" (334). His reaction is, for a moment at least, supportive, but then "he was asking her what she wanted to do about it." Spencer provides her reflections: "It was not an unnatural question; it was, in fact, the most natural question in the world. It was just that even the thought of what he might be getting to drove her wild. She didn't want to think about it yet, even to know as regards her own and Jake's child that the possibility of such a 'solution' had ever been mentioned or even dreamed of" (334). She leaps up in despair and runs from him, straight toward a huge black Cadillac that has been circling the square. Straight toward Ted Marnie.

There is a subtle irony in this scene. As sympathetic as Jake Springland may have been to Julia's announcement, Spencer's readers are even more so. By this point in the novel, they are more intimate with her emotional life than he is, having witnessed her slowly growing need for children and stability during "the in-between years." If readers have by this point developed the relationship with Julia Garrett that Spencer intends, they are horrified to see her dragged by force down into the vortex of corruption at the precise moment when new life is beginning within her. For the reader, like Jake Springland, has no idea Julia is pregnant until the moment before she is kidnapped.

Later, when Julia sees the dead Marnie floating in the bottom of a well, it confirms in her what the kidnapping scene first suggests to the reader—the pattern of *The Snare*. Julia's life spirals downward in a slowly tightening gyre through cycles of relationships and growing insight. It strikes the emotional center of evil at its lowest point, her kidnapping and debasement at the hands of Ted Marnie, who becomes her own private Satan frozen at the center of her world.[8]

8. As Woodland suggests, this pattern certainly has strong allusions to Dante, not the least of which is the necessity of experiencing evil before spiritual elevation is possible. Despite the consistent reference to Baudelaire in the novel, it may well be that Dante is an even more significant influence. See Woodland, " 'In That City Foreign and Paradoxical.' "

It is no accident, then, that Julia Garrett's life begins to spiral upward within her at the point when she experiences pure evil. Having experienced "the worst that could happen" both within her world and within herself, she is now equipped for a new cycle of life—resurrection and regeneration.

After Marnie's death and the final disappearance of Springland, Julia Garrett bears her baby son, Emile, and then drifts into an informal, slow-paced relationship with Tommy Arnold, recently divorced. Although at the end of the novel they have not moved in together, nor have they resolved the question of marriage, the very ease with which they approach these decisions suggests a permanence, a stability in two lives that had before been unhappily hectic. What the three—man, woman, child—achieve without bothering to name it is the communion that Julia had finally discovered as essential. After she and Springland had broken bread with the other, mostly black and Creole members of his jazz ensemble, she had realized that a completely *shared* life is what she had missed since Dev's death: "From that time on she knew the truth: happiness is communion. Why had it taken her so long to find it? She remembered once some weeks back seeing Edie and Paul Fowler in their station wagon, baby carriage and picnic hamper, the whole bit, stopped at a drive-in grocery before the outing, and how she'd curbed her impulse to go and greet them, how something had appalled her about it all, the sight of American coziness. . . .Well, how would *I* do it? she wondered, turning away depressed. Not that way, she thought" (324).

How she will do it is Spencer's concern in the last forty-eight pages of the novel, in the section entitled "Battle." This is an apt title for the finish of a Spencer heroine's story because after years of external violence and instability, Julia's last battle is primarily an internal one. What she battles against is her self—her own secretiveness, her own lack of trust in herself and others. Ultimately what she must do is reveal herself, all of her crooked as well as straight tendencies to Arnold, the man most like her. He too, she realizes, had gotten "all the way to the dead center when [he] finally got divorced" and has failed to climb back into life (365). Her affection and acceptance revive him, however, and she in loving him teaches him the ultimate lesson of all her long trial. When she finally is able to tell him about the horrors of Marnie and Springland, Arnold tries to restrain her.

"Stop it! Stop it now! Wipe it out, Julia."

"That's the worst thing of all," she said calmly, after a long pause. "To say that is worse than anything. No, I'll have it, Tommy. All of it. I'll not refuse any part of it. . . . The joy's in that, Tommy. In not refusing." (402)

This, then, is her final realization, that the corruption must be acknowledged before the love will flow.

Although there is no direct reference in *The Snare* to Yeats, there is in Julia Garret much of the same divine madness that makes up the Irish poet's "Crazy Jane." In "Crazy Jane Talks with the Bishop," an earlier exchange in the long conversation between the straight and crooked worlds, Yeats's Jane closes the argument by admitting that

> A woman can be proud and stiff
> When on love intent.
> But Love has pitched his mansion in
> The place of excrement;
> For nothing can be sole or whole
> That has not been rent.[9]

Having both "been rent," Julia Garrett and Tommy Arnold finally seek wholeness together. "They were, of course, happy, these old acquaintances, happy and lazy. What they argued about, what they decided—it didn't matter much" (373). The communion they discover exists because they now accept themselves whole. Having "been rent," they accept both the best and worst in themselves and in each other.

If *The Snare* is read as a Spencerian detective story, what Julia Garrett stalks is ultimately not death but a life freed from the fear of death. It concerns the spiritual basis of self-acceptance and self-knowledge. It concerns the spiritual basis of a true communion that can exist, Julia discovers, in her own haunted New Orleans. Although Spencer's focus appears to have shifted from that of her earlier novels, her primary concern is still the same. What had begun twenty-four years and six novels before as a fascination with *community*—small Mississippi towns saturated in family—has evolved into a fascination with *communion*—the inner lives of broken people seeking wholeness. What she conveys with the technical virtuosity of *The Snare* is that emotional wholeness in human relations is directly tied to emotional wholeness within those involved. She creates in

9. William Butler Yeats, "Crazy Jane Talks with the Bishop," in Yeats, *The Poems: A New Edition*, ed. Richard J. Finneran (New York, 1983), 259–60.

her imagined New Orleans a reflection of her heroine's inner life so that she can capture the depth and complexity of both simultaneously. The fabric of Julia's emotional life is rent time and again, as is the community around her; her life resurrects itself within her as the life she shares with others reknits itself.

The Snare represents the culmination of several of Spencer's artistic quests. She is able with Julia Garrett as her protagonist to convey the complexity of an external community at the same time she conveys the complexity of an internal search for communion. Since the sudden change in artistic direction after *The Light in the Piazza*, Spencer had grappled in her long fiction with the technical problems involved in portraying at once two worlds, external and internal. She discovered the solution in Julia Garrett, a figure who is both a compendium of her external world and a very real woman "who could take it and survive." Her survival suggests that Spencer has also solved the psychological conundrum facing all her characters from Martha Ingram on—how to maintain nurturing relations in a broken world. The characters of *No Place for an Angel*, for example, find love an impossibility. It is not until *The Snare* that Spencer discovers a place for her particular angel, communion, in New Orleans. What she discovers through Julia Garrett is that external communion requires internal harmony and that internal harmony requires the full recognition of both voices, "one . . . love and the other corruption."

In her most recent description of *The Snare*, Spencer returned to language she had used years before to describe *No Place for an Angel*. There are "layers of discovery" in Julia Garrett's life, she said, "all of which are playing in a . . . symphonic way with the city of New Orleans."[10] Unfortunately, *The Snare*, Spencer's finest achievement, has yet to find the audience its symphonic richness deserves.

10. Roberts, "Whole Personality," in *Conversations with Elizabeth Spencer*, ed. Prenshaw, 228.

7 / A Certain Path, a Personal Road

I think many of the stories are about liberation and the regret you have when you liberate yourself.

When I look back [at *Jack of Diamonds*] I see there is a related theme. Perhaps it is mystery in close relationships.

—Elizabeth Spencer, in interviews

The publication in 1981 of *The Stories of Elizabeth Spencer* marked a reversal in Spencer's critical fortunes.[1] Her previous two novels, *No Place for an Angel* and *The Snare*, had brought her insensitive and increasingly unfavorable reviews as well as declining sales. The appearance of the volume of stories dramatically revived Spencer's reputation. Reviewers, including writers James Dickey and Reynolds Price, lavished praise on the volume, and in 1983, Spencer received the Award of Merit Medal for the Short Story from the American Academy and Institute of Arts and Letters. The publication of five later stories under the title *Jack of Diamonds* in 1988 was widely taken as further proof of her mastery of the form.[2] The widespread response to her short fiction revived an interest in her previously published novels and set the stage for *The Salt Line* (1984).

But the collection of these thirty-three stories in one volume did

1. The collection contains the ten stories collected earlier as *Ship Island and Other Stories* (1968) and the novella *Knights and Dragons* (1965) as well as twenty-two other not previously collected stories. Several of these stories first appeared in Canadian periodicals and were often anthologized in Canada. Also in 1981, the University Press of Mississippi brought out *Marilee*, a small collection of the three stories narrated by Marilee Summerall.
2. See, for example, Madison Smartt Bell's review in the *New York Times Book Review* of September 4, 1988.

more than bring renewed attention to Spencer's long fiction; it also shed light on the development of that fiction. The stories appear in the order in which they were written (not published), reflecting, Spencer writes in her preface, her image of herself "walking down a certain path, a personal road." Reading the short stories in order and in the context of the novels suggests that Spencer's "personal road" might be profitably divided into four sections.

Spencer's organization of the stories into four chronological groups implies this pattern, which in turn reflects clearly the development of theme and technique in the novels. The first section of stories consists of those early pieces set in rural Mississippi and written between 1944 and 1960, the time of the early Mississippi novels. The stories of the second period (1961–1964) are set in Italy as well as in the South, suggesting immediately the two Italian novellas, one of which Spencer includes in this part of the collection. The stories of the second section suggest a more fragmented world view, with characters troubled, restless, out of their natural element. Spencer worked alternately on both *No Place for an Angel* and *The Snare* during the third period reflected here (1965–1971), and the stories of that time mirror first the nihilism and then the slowly growing spiritual reconciliation found in those two novels.

The stories of the fourth section plus the five stories of *Jack of Diamonds* (1972–1987) are the products of Spencer's mature period and probe how the psyches of her characters both form and are formed by their relations with others. Ultimately, two important patterns emerge in a study of these stories: first, a period of technical experimentation followed by technical mastery; and second, disillusionment and dislocation followed by reconciliation and "something like acceptance, the affirming of what is not an especially perfect world for these seeking girls and women."[3] The acceptance of "not an especially perfect world" recalls *The Snare* and anticipates *The Salt Line*. The word *acceptance* is important to Spencer in this metaphysical context. It suggests a kind of spiritual faith in the way things are that is crucial to her mature sensibility. She uses the same term to denote the heroine's response to a teeming world in "The Day Before," one of only a few autobiographical stories she has written: "I knew that if I lived to be a thousand I would never do anything but *accept* it if an old man fed his dogs out of the best china or if a parrot could

3. Spencer, preface to *The Stories of Elizabeth Spencer*, xi.

quote Shakespeare."[4] The theme of acceptance also completes the pattern of displacement and reconciliation suggested by the short fiction, a pattern that sheds much light on the novels.

The stories from the earliest period are all, with the exception of the last ("The White Azalea"), set in Mississippi. They tend to focus on a young protagonist engaged in discovering "his or her separation from" a loved one and "the concomitant sense of loss and freedom."[5] Like *Fire in the Morning* and *The Voice at the Back Door* from the same period, Spencer narrates these stories omnisciently with the action flowing more or less uninterruptedly from one point in time forward to another. The single exception to this generalization is the first of the Marilee stories, "Southern Landscape," which, though narrated in the first person, is still quite traditional in technique. Representative of these stories is the often-anthologized "First Dark" (1959).

Set in the small fictional town of Richton, Mississippi, "First Dark" concerns the power of the past to ensnare the lives of contemporary men and women. The title refers to the point in the evening when the town's ghost regularly appears. Tom Beavers has moved away from Richton to Jackson but visits home regularly to maintain contact with his past, to avoid seeing his life "cut in two." When he explains this to Frances Harvey, a young woman he meets there, she warns him: "There's more than one ghost in Richton. You may turn into one like the rest of us" (28). Frances Harvey's involvement with Tom Beavers forces her to decide between a life with him and a life nursing her ancient mother in the Harvey mansion. "I can't leave her, Tom," she tells him. "But I can't ask you to live with her, either. . . . You'd hate me in a week" (34). This dilemma is resolved when Mrs. Harvey dies suddenly. Frances, however, suspects her mother has committed suicide to set her free. There is much more to this narrative than a Faulknerian mansion and a proud old belle, however. Frances Harvey is suspended precariously between the past and any possible future and is in grave danger of herself becoming a ghost: "In Richton, the door to the past was always wide open, and what came in through it and went out of it had made people 'different.'

4. *The Stories of Elizabeth Spencer* (Garden City, N.Y., 1981), 229 (my emphasis). Hereinafter cited by page number in the text.
5. Prenshaw, *Elizabeth Spencer*, 133.

But it scarcely ever happens, even in Richton, that one is able to see the precise moment when fact becomes faith, when life turns into legend, and people start to bend their finest loyalties to make themselves bemused custodians of the grave. Tom Beavers saw that moment now, in the profile of this dreaming girl, and he knew there was no time to lose" (39).

Realizing that he must defeat the past gathering around Frances, Tom takes her away the same evening he learns of her mother's suicide, leaving the old house "to enter with abandon the land of mourning and shadows and memory" (40). Frances Harvey is as sensitive as Marcia Mae Hunt (from *The Voice at the Back Door*) to the iron ties of family and tradition, but she lacks Marcia Mae's strength of will. It takes another human bond—the romantic tie to Beavers—to wrench her free of life as an invalid in time.

The other central story of the section, "A Southern Landscape" (1960), is the first of the three Marilee stories, and in it Marilee's warm, wise nature and playful voice take the reader by the arm from the opening line: "If you're like me and sometimes turn through the paper reading anything and everything because you're too lazy to get up and do what you ought to be doing, then you already know about my hometown" (41). Her story proves her point. For this landscape, though it reeks of verisimilitude, is not a literal one. Marilee is reciting the events of her senior year in high school from memory at a distance of some years. The story centers around her slapstick romance with the alcohol-soaked Foster Hamilton, a highly entertaining but also highly frustrating older beau. Marilee's compelling voice and the distance from which she tells her story establish long before the closing lines that this is a "landscape of the heart" rather than of the road map. As Spencer wrote in her preface to the collected Marilee stories, "It's the voice you talk about it with that makes the difference."[6] Marilee's voice served Spencer for a period bridging twenty-eight years and three stories. It has proved to be her entrée into the South of her childhood not because it is autobiographical but because it allows Marilee—and through her, Spencer—to re-create rural Mississippi as an emotional landmark. "I feel the need," admits the mature Marilee Summerall, "of a land, of a sure terrain, of a sort of permanent landscape of the heart" (52). This first

6. Elizabeth Spencer, preface to Spencer, *Marilee* (Jackson, 1981), 8.

Marilee story, then, is not so much about the past as it is what the artistic sensibility does with the past. In this way, it provides an early key to Spencer's own artistic development.

The next stage in that development is one of expansion, both in setting and technique. Both are anticipated by the final story in the first section of the collection, "The White Azalea" (1961). In it, middle-aged Miss Theresa Stubblefield of Tuxapoka, Alabama, has finally escaped years of servitude "nursing various Stubblefields . . . through their lengthy illnesses" and made her way to Rome. On the day of her arrival, she discovers two letters waiting at the American Express office, one describing a death in the family and the other dropping broad hints that she return immediately to take matters in hand. "The trouble is," Theresa thinks, "that while everything that happens there is supposed to matter supremely, nothing here is supposed to even exist" (67). After some moments of angry soul-searching, Theresa tears up the two letters and then buries them neatly in the pot of a huge white azalea placed near her by Italian workmen. She is quite conscious of the symbolism ("It was not the letters but the Stubblefields that she had torn open and consigned to the earth" [69]), even thrilled by it, and her victory over her family is a significant one.

Theresa's rejection of the Stubblefields and Tuxapoka signals Spencer's expanding sensibility in two ways. Obviously, Theresa Stubblefield has opened up for herself and Spencer the world of *The Light in the Piazza* and *Knights and Dragons*, an exotic, complex social arena. Even more important, however, is Spencer's emphasis on Theresa's inner life, the psychological drama that precedes her destruction of the letters. Although the story is narrated omnisciently, Spencer centers the narrative presence in Theresa's mind and outlook, anticipating the technical dilemmas Spencer faced in her two Italian novellas. The tension between the inner reality of Theresa's memories of Tuxapoka and the outer reality of Romans preparing for a floral festival is palpable. Spencer's careful balancing of the two also mirrors the novels of the period, particularly *The Light in the Piazza*.

Despite its affinities with the stories of Spencer's second period, "The White Azalea" does not prepare the reader for the existential dilemmas that will face Spencer's heroines in those stories. For example, "The Visit," "Ship Island," and "The Pincian Gate" are similar to *Knights and Dragons* (which Spencer included in the *Stories*), in that their protagonists experience a fundamental displacement from their worlds.

"Ship Island" (1964) is an especially important story because it introduces for the first time the Spencer heroine who is out of her element, a topic that will continue to fascinate the author. In 1982, Spencer told J. G. Jones that "Ship Island" was a story that "started a new theme in my work. . . . It's that women feel themselves very often imprisoned by what people expect of them [and] . . . some . . . mount rebellion: they are not going to put up with it."[7] The subtitle of the piece, "The Story of a Mermaid," is a key to the imagery Spencer uses to define the protagonist, Nancy Lewis. She is out of sync with both her own family and the socially affluent group of her boyfriend, Rob Acklen. She is at home only in or near the ocean, specifically on Ship Island. She feels painfully out of place in the restaurants, bars, and expensive homes haunted by Rob and his friends, however, and at a key juncture she abandons Rob in a restaurant to leave with several mysterious men.

Taken at face value, her impetuous decision seems dangerously irrational. But Spencer has foreshadowed it from early in the story with the sea imagery she associates with Nancy, who, the narrator tells us, was "hearing the right things said to her and Rob, and smiling back at the right things but longing to jump off into the dark as if it were water. The dark, with the moon mixed in with it, seemed to her like good deep water to go off in" (99).

After she sets off for New Orleans with her two mystery men, she again feels the pull of the ocean: "Nancy watched the point where the moon actually met the water. It was moving and still at once. She thought that it was glorious, in a messy sort of way. She would have liked to poke her head up out of the water right there. She could feel the water pouring back through her white-blond hair, her face slathering over with moonlight" (106). Confronted by Rob upon her return from New Orleans, she again feels herself drawing away emotionally: "Her voice faded in a deepening glimmer where the human breath is snatched clean away and there are only bubbles, iridescent and pure. When she dove again, they rose in a curving track behind her" (110).

Spencer uses this imagery to establish Nancy's growing sense of

---

7. John Griffin Jones, "Elizabeth Spencer," in *Conversations with Elizabeth Spenser,* ed. Prenshaw, 97.

herself as a creature of a different order than Rob or her family. She can hardly breathe in their element and must turn elsewhere for emotional nourishment. In both her use of imagery to further Nancy's story and her use of the Gulf coast as a setting for surreal action, Spencer anticipates *The Salt Line*. More important, however, she signals her growing interest in characters who are radically misplaced in their social settings. This is the beginning of a long artistic quest for Spencer—a search for the nature of true community and the narrative techniques with which to portray it.

The last story in the second section, "The Pincian Gate" (1966), shares the Italian setting of its contemporary novels while at the same time mirroring their technical experimentation. This brief tale (less than six pages in the *Stories*) is a masterpiece of controlled irony. An American woman living in Rome is visiting an American artist who lives within the Roman wall near the Pincio. Spencer confines the omniscient point of view largely to the woman's perspective, and so it is through her that we learn that she, Sara, and her husband, Paul, intend to remind artist Gowan Palmer of opportunities—"financial, emotional, artistic, and otherwise"—that he should take advantage of (121). Caught by her seemingly good intentions, the reader sympathizes with her growing irritation as Palmer playfully ridicules her concerns. "She felt the rug pulled out from under" her arguments, and "she was angry enough to wonder if she would ever really want to see him again at all" (124, 125). As she is leaving in a huff, Palmer suddenly "turned her face abruptly to his and gave her a long staggering kiss," which shatters both her and the readers' illusions simultaneously (125–26). A glance back through the story reveals the clues that were there from the first paragraph; his independence is necessary to his calling, and her concern is only pointless meddling. Spencer's manipulation of Sara's limited point of view is masterly in its use of irony. It both reflects the technical problems raised by Spencer's growing interest in internal reality and foreshadows the technical mastery of *No Place for an Angel* and *The Snare*.

Although these two novels were published five years apart, "many scenes . . . were written for each before I finished either," Spencer said, and together they mark off the third period of her story writing.[8] While the pain and disillusionment of these two novels are reflected in stories such as "Judith Kane," "The Finder," and "Instru-

8. Spencer, preface to *The Stories of Elizabeth Spencer*, x.

ment of Destruction," the reconciliation present at the core of *The Snare* is also present—in stories such as "The Day Before," "Presents," "On the Gulf," and "Sharon." Spencer's return to an obviously southern setting for nine of the thirteen stories in this section (written mostly in Canada) suggests more than the nostalgia she mentions in the preface. Her southern characters from this section, including Marilee Summerall, tend to discover communal humor and nourishment in their "landscapes of the heart." Through the power of her imagination, Spencer has shaped for herself and her readers a reconciliation with the South that her characters had previously rejected.

One of the finest of Spencer's stories from this or any period, "The Finder" (1971), illustrates this conflict between acceptance and rejection of the southern setting. It begins: "Dalton was such a pleasant town—still is. Lots of shade trees on residential streets, lots of shrubs in all the front yards, ferns in tubs put outside in the summer, birdbaths well attended, and screen side porches with familiar voices going on through the twilight. Crêpe myrtle lined the uptown streets" (291).

The protagonist, Gavin Anderson, belongs to one of the oldest, most influential families in town and is so deeply integrated into family and communal life that he has developed an extrasensory perception. He has the supernatural ability to find lost things. He retains his gift as he matures, marries, and becomes a father, all the while growing more deeply a part of his family and community. He meets and becomes involved with a young widow, Naomi Beris, for whom he "finds" a lost ruby ring. Attracted by her cosmopolitan sensuality, so alien to his life in Dalton, he sleeps with her and, for a time at least, loses his gift. Symbolically, he has forsaken his place at the "eternal table" of the Anderson family and lost his perfect sense of his surroundings (304).[9] Alarmed, he ends the affair and reconciles with his wife.

The story seems about to draw to a predictable close, but as Gavin is driving along a gravel road, he suddenly becomes through the power of his gift the long-dead lover of Naomi's grandmother. What had seemed resolved, finished, suddenly explodes in the last lines of the story. Anderson's gift, which had tied him so intimately to Dalton

9. Gavin's sense of the Andersons as "one long table of a family" echoes Julia Garrett's discovery of "communion" in *The Snare*. In each instance, Spencer uses the ritually shared meal to symbolize communal intimacy.

and his family, suddenly lifts him violently out of both. His gift is analogous in its power and precision to Marilee Summerall's re-creative voice and, by extension, the artistic imagination itself. Anderson discovers that the gift of artistic sensibility is both a curse and a blessing; it both integrates its bearer into the communion of shared life and simultaneously renders that communion unbearably intimate. The story's powerful ending does not resolve this dilemma for Gavin Anderson, because the story is less about the man that it is about his gift.

Spencer's second Marilee story, "Sharon" (1970), was written just prior to "The Finder" and is fueled by the same conflict of attraction to and repulsion from home and family. This story expands Marilee's familial context to include her Uncle Hernan, her "mother's brother (his full name is Hernando de Soto Wirth)," and his farm home, Sharon (281). The action occurs prior to that of "Southern Landscape." Marilee is still a preadolescent girl. She is a favorite of her uncle's and is regularly invited to Sharon for the noon meal. This meal is prepared by Uncle Hernan's cook and housekeeper, a young black woman named Melissa, who had come to Sharon as the personal maid of Hernan's long-dead wife. Marilee enjoys these meals and her conversations with Uncle Hernan, but she is taught by her parents that she "could never . . . go over to Uncle Hernan's without being asked . . . [which] became, of course, the apple in the garden" (288). Despite her mother's evident dislike of Melissa, Marilee finally gives into temptation and crosses over to Sharon unannounced. What she sees through the parlor window is her Uncle Hernan and Melissa together in the relaxed intimacy of a couple long used to each other. Suddenly the young Marilee and the reader reach the conclusion that the older narrative presence has staged for them. Melissa's children, "perfect little devils" every one, are Marilee's cousins. This realization opens to her suddenly the breadth and depth of her own family and her own tradition: "That blood was ours, mingling and twining with the other. Mama could kick like a mule, fight like a wildcat in a sack, but she would never get it out. It was there for good" (290).

Spencer ends this second Marilee narrative with a pun; the phrase "for good" means both "forever" and "for the benefit of all." The young Marilee Summerall understands the first of these two meanings immediately; it requires the maturity of the older narrator to perceive the second. At the close of this central story, Spencer manages to capture both the daunting complexity of her southern heritage and her growing acceptance of it—in a single phrase.

Part of Spencer's reconciliation with the South as a fictional landscape stems from her relationship with the Gulf coast. Spencer herself has commented on her particularly sensitive response to the spirituality of place. "Place is sacred," she said in 1990. "There's a spirit . . . to be worshipped or violated." And no place is more spiritually alive for Spencer than the Gulf coast. In the preface to a 1991 collection of her previously published Gulf coast stories, Spencer describes the first time she walked across Ship Island and saw the open Gulf: "I saw it there before me, what I'd come for without knowing it: the true Gulf, no horizon to curb its expanse, spread out infinite and free, restless with tossing white caps, rushing to foam up the beach, retreating, returning, roaring. Out there I thought, astonished, is Mexico, the Caribbean, South America. We are leaning outward to them. Everybody back there on land, all along the coast, feels this presence, whether they consciously know it or not. What was it but the distance, the leaning outward, the opening toward far-off, unlikely worlds? The beyond."[10]

In contrast, she writes, the inland towns of her childhood contained "a complex and at times beautiful society . . . but the smell of salt air did not reach it, and none can deny that it was confined and confining."[11] The 1968 story "On the Gulf" illustrates in its light and breezy playfulness exactly this tone of openness and freedom that Spencer found in Gulf coast culture. Furthermore, these two passages from the preface to *On the Gulf* contain the key to much of Spencer's creative life of the late 1960s and early 1970s. In order to reconcile herself with the "confined and confining" South as a fictional subject, she used two methods. The first was the artistic distance provided by Marilee Summerall and other artist figures. The second, more powerful entrée was the spiritual acceptance Spencer discovered in exploring the Gulf coast as a "permanent landscape" of the spirit.

Spencer's use of the supernatural in stories such as "The Finder" and in the later novel *The Salt Line* is also characteristic of this third

10. Roberts, "Whole Personality," in *Conversations with Elizabeth Spencer,* ed. Prenshaw, 221; Elizabeth Spencer, preface to Spencer, *On the Gulf* (Jackson, 1991), xvii.

11. Spencer, preface to Spencer, *On the Gulf,* xix.

period in her career, that of reconciliation.[12] Her admittedly intense response to the "spirituality of place" may in fact be the key to understanding her imaginative return to the sea and landscape of the southern stories of these years, which culminated in *The Salt Line*.[13]

The stories of the fourth period of her career continue the pattern of growing objectivity about the South combined with a masterly range of setting and narrative technique. A glance at the contents pages of *The Stories of Elizabeth Spencer* and *Jack of Diamonds* reveals both her renewed interest in the South as well as her range; seven of the thirteen stories collected since 1972 have distinctly southern settings, four are set in Canada, one in New England, and one, "Port of Embarkation," in an unidentified locale.

She takes as her theme in this mature period the deeper "mystery in close relationships," a continuation of her lifelong fascination with community and intimacy.[14] In many ways, the stories of this period suggest both *The Snare*, with its frightening examination of the evil inherent in human relations, and *The Salt Line*, with its magical healing of evil's destructive wounds. Although in some of these stories—such as "I, Maureen," "Jack of Diamonds," "The Business Venture," and "The Skater"—the predominant tone is one of unsettled darkness, there is in the majority of them a stronger sense of reconciliation and recovery. They also reflect the technical range and maturity of *The Snare* and *The Salt Line*; in them Spencer writes with precision and power in an impressive array of first-person and limited-omniscient voices, focusing on a wide variety of both male and female characters.

The evolution of Spencer's mature power in the short story is

12. Elsa Nettels recently observed that Spencer's stories "highlight the most distinctive quality of [her] fiction: the emanation . . . of mysterious forces"—a comment that reflects Spencer's growing use of the supernatural during this period. Elsa Nettels, "Elizabeth Spencer" in *Southern Women Writers: The New Generation*, ed. Tonette Bond Inge (Tuscaloosa, 1990), 91–92.

13. See my 1990 interview with Spencer—"Whole Personality," in *Conversations with Elizabeth Spencer*, ed. Prenshaw, esp. 220–21. It may be that Spencer required a *spiritual* reconciliation because she had earlier rejected the stringent Calvinism of her parents and Carrollton. She has suggested that "A Christian Education," which treats this topic, is one of her few autobiographical stories. Her spiritual response to the Gulf coast may have been necessary to counteract her distaste for the "confined and confining" southern religion she attacks in *This Crooked Way*.

14. Robert Phillips, "Mystery in Close Relationships: An Interview with Elizabeth Spencer," in *Conversations with Elizabeth Spencer*, ed. Prenshaw, 181–85.

suggested immediately by the third and most recent of the Marilee stories, "Indian Summer," first published in 1978. In it, Marilee recounts the struggles of her Uncle Rex (Hernan's brother) to overcome the emotional problems created by his marriage. He had given up a wild youth to marry into a staid but powerful family and had come eventually to farm his wife's family property, which he did not own. His lack of patrimony and of the legitimacy it would suggest "galls him," as Uncle Hernan correctly discerns (381). Confronted by his wife and grown son over a real estate decision, he quits farm and family in disgust, taking only his favorite riding mare in a trailer pulled behind his pickup.[15]

Rex disappears from sight, eventually to be discovered living in the Delta in an informal household with a much younger woman and her son. Marilee spies on him there from a distant vantage point, watching this impromptu family through binoculars: "There is such a thing as father, daughter, and grandchild—such a thing as family that is not blood family but a chosen family. I was seeing that. . . . Now, not needing glasses, or eyes, either, I see the problem Rex Wirth must be solving and unsolving every day. If this was the place he belonged and the family that was—though not of blood—in a sense, his, why leave them ever? . . . Wasn't this where he belonged? . . . Should I run out of the woods and tell him that? No, the struggle was his own" (398).

This passage is significant in a number of ways. First, Spencer places her ever present concern with community—"blood family" versus "chosen family"—at the heart of the story. It is the "problem Rex Wirth must be solving and unsolving every day." It is also the problem that Marilee is "solving and unsolving" as she narrates these stories about the Wirths, her own blood family *and* the family she chooses through the act of telling. Here Marilee's growing objectivity in relation to her subject is also important.

In "A Southern Landscape" she is both narrator and protagonist;

---

15. In the stories from the 1970s, Spencer often uses a spirited horse to symbolize the individual spirit. At the end of "A Christian Education," it is "the bright horse of freedom . . . already loose in [the narrator's] world" (331). In "The Girl Who Loved Horses" (1979), Deborah Mecklin's growth from early independence to later maturity is symbolized by her relations to and attitude toward horses. In "Port of Embarkation" (1977), the emotional struggle of the twelve-year-old narrator's family is represented in her early dream of a team of horses, one shorter than the other, pulling a "heavily laden wagon" up a hill (407).

the external as well as the internal action center around her. In "Sharon" the external focus is on the mystique of Sharon, where the enigmatic Uncle Hernan lives with his black common-law wife. While the internal development is obviously Marilee's, she is no longer the subject of her own scrutiny. In "Indian Summer" Marilee is even further removed from the action, literally as far from a parlor window to a distant hilltop and emotionally to the distance from which she can realize that Rex's struggle is his own, not hers. This trilogy of Marilee stories illustrates Marilee's removal from the center of external action to the point of observer and interpreter of that action for the reader.

The trilogy also serves as a microcosm of the entire collection by illustrating how this increasing objectivity in the narrative persona is part of a larger process, Spencer's growing technical mastery.[16] Whereas both "A Southern Landscape" and "Sharon" are relatively straightforward first-person memoirs, "Indian Summer" jumps backward and forward in time and draws on a number of indirect encounters and even imagined conversations and repeated dreams. Although it is as accessible and engaging as the earlier stories—the sign of Spencer's mature craft—it is a much more complex narrative.

The same is true of almost all of the stories of Spencer's fourth, most mature period. They are the most complex and at the same time most successful of her career. In them she explores the nature of identity as it is revealed by the demands of intimacy. Whereas earlier she had responded to a question about the 1981 collection by saying they were about "liberation and the regret you have when you liberate yourself," she said of the 1988 *Jack of Diamonds* that its recurrent theme was the larger, more complex "mystery in close relationships."[17] Two of the stories from this period set in Canada illustrate how rich and complicated is this mystery.

The heroine of "Jean-Pierre," the first story in *Jack of Diamonds*, marries a mysterious French Canadian. A year after their wedding, her husband disappears for several months suddenly and with no explanation. Having rejected her family for Jean-Pierre, Callie is abandoned to life alone in an unfamiliar part of the city. She gets a

16. It is impossible to say whether Spencer's gradual acceptance of modern experience and reconciliation with the southern landscape was the *cause* or the *result* of her maturing craft; even so, it is certain that the two processes are vitally connected.

17. Broadwell and Hoag, "Conversation," and Phillips, "Mystery in Close Relationships," both in *Conversations with Elizabeth Spencer*, ed. Prenshaw, 56, 177.

job in a library, begins to read Emily Dickinson, and befriends a lonely young married man. She and her new friend travel one day to New England, partly in search of the magic of Dickinson. There, they discover an abandoned, flooded-out rock quarry, which Callie recognizes as "the atom's tomb" described by Dickinson.[18] Analogous to the abandoned well that Julia Garrett discovers at her lowest point in *The Snare*, the quarry is the spot where Callie turns instinctively back to her husband.[19] When Callie and her friend arrive back in Montreal, Jean-Pierre has returned, as if in response to her deepest affirmation of their union. "Jean-Pierre" introduces Spencer's emphasis on the mysterious in human relations; Callie and Jean-Pierre barely know each other, are mismatched in age and culture, struggle constantly with the language, and yet know intuitively that they belong together. Their reunion reverses the emphasis on displacement in stories such as "Ship Island" and "I, Maureen," another Canadian story from the mature period.

"I, Maureen" (1976), with its echo of *I, Claudius*, is in the last section of the 1981 collection. Like "Jean-Pierre," it echoes *The Snare*, but in different ways. In it, the narrator, Maureen, marries into one of the richest families in Montreal and bears children to a caring husband. Maureen's ultimate reaction against her perfect life is even stronger than Julia Garrett's antipathy for Martin Parham's familial wealth.[20] Here Spencer essays several experimental techniques to suggest Maureen's brush with insanity. She is torn between her attraction to her children and husband and her abject fear of the subtle manipulation that life with them entails. To dramatize her all-but-psychotic turmoil, Spencer blurs her fantasies into their peculiar perceptions of the world, capturing powerfully Maureen's desperate need for some reconciliation of the psychological forces that tear her. Her narrative dramatizes the degree to which her

18. Elizabeth Spencer, *Jack of Diamonds* (New York, 1988), 23. Hereinafter cited by page number in the text.

19. Like "Jean-Pierre," "The Girl Who Loved Horses" (the last story in the 1981 volume) reflects the basic pattern of *The Snare*. In each story, a young woman is brought face to face with her deepest and most dangerous doubts and desires. Deborah Mecklin, "the girl who loved horses," even courts violence and depravity much like Julia Garrett. In each instance, the protagonist recovers from her flirtation with "the atom's tomb" to accept the life-affirming complexities of communal life. For Deborah Mecklin, this means motherhood; for Callie, a return to a difficult marriage.

20. Maureen is married to *Denis Partham*, obviously a reincarnation of Julia Garrett's *Martin Parham*.

personality all but splits into actor and observer. Spencer even suggests typographically this split; when Maureen introduces herself in the first line of the story, it is as "I (Maureen)," emphasizing the subconscious distinction between the two. From that point on, most of her references to herself involve her splitting the first-person pronoun from her name with some sort of punctuation, thus unconsciously splitting her persona.[21] The text of the story itself is unsettling in its syntactic displacement, mirroring the surrealism of Maureen's perspective. Compared with the earlier *Knights and Dragons*, "I, Maureen" is more polished, more accessible, and more dramatic, even though it takes the reader deeper into Maureen's personality through her first-person voice.[22] Here again is evidence of Spencer's growing power to dramatize even the deeply disturbed personality.

Elsa Nettels' insightful comment that "life and death, health and sickness, sanity and madness are inseparable in Elizabeth Spencer's world" is primarily true of her later fiction.[23] This inseparability of vital but opposing forces accounts for the insoluble mystery at the core of human relationships. As a result, there is a largely unresolved tension in these mature stories, whether the protagonist accepts the mystery as his or her own or seeks to ignore it. Two Mississippi stories from *Jack of Diamonds*, "The Business Venture" and "The Cousins," illustrate these opposing reactions—one life-denying and the other life-affirming.

The title of "The Business Venture" refers to an attempt by a southern white woman, Nelle Townshend, to open a dry-cleaning business in a small town. Complications arise—she turns away from her former close circle of friends, neighbors complain of the chemical odors from her machinery—all of which stem from the fact that her business partner is a black man. At first glance it appears that the

21. Maureen's dilemma as both actor in and teller of her own tale is even more obvious when compared with that other well-known Spencer narrator, Marilee Summerall. Marilee's supreme confidence in her power to reshape and reconcile the complex forces of her own family life contrasts sharply with that of her northern cousin. Their names suggest, as those of Spencer's characters often do, that their author means this comparison to be made.

22. In his review, Reynolds Price found in *Knights and Dragons* a "Jamesian murk in both style and statement" but praised the "all clear and calm" control of "I, Maureen." Reynolds Price, "The Art of American Short Stories" *New York Times Book Review*, March 1, 1981, p. 1.

23. Nettels, "Elizabeth Spencer," in *Southern Women Writers*, ed. Inge, 94.

story concerns the turmoil caused by their friendship in the small southern town. However, there is an even more significant subplot intertwined with that of the dry-cleaning business. Eileen Waybridge, who narrates the story, has with her husband, Charlie, always run in the same close group with Nelle Townshend. During the course of the events she describes, Eileen comes to sympathize with Nelle's desire to escape the close confines of their circle of friends, particularly as Eileen's efforts to rein in her philandering husband repeatedly fail. At the story's close, she accidentally overhears Charlie threaten Nelle over the telephone and realizes suddenly that it is Nelle among others that he has been seeing all along. In shock, she realizes that in their web of precarious relationships, they "are all hanging on a golden thread," without knowing "who has got the other end" (159). At this point, she comes into focus as the protagonist of the story, and her last confession—"I'm praying that it holds us all suspended"—echoes beyond the end of the story itself. It is an unsettling, ominous ending to what had seemed for some pages a social comedy.

If in the balance of optimism and pessimism, acceptance and denial, "The Business Venture" tips the scales toward despair, "The Cousins" rights those scales again. "The Cousins" is a long, first-person narrative told by the fifty-year-old Ella Mason, who recalls for the reader a trip she made to Europe thirty years before with two of her male cousins and some other friends. During the trip, she had fallen in love with her second cousin Eric, but after an idyllic few days, they had been split by the disturbing news that he did not get into law school. In the story's present, she is on her way to Italy to visit Eric for a long-postponed reunion. The story line shifts back and forth between present and past, developing the two subplots in a counterpoint rhythm, leading inevitably to the discovery and loss of intimacy in the past and to the opportunity for its recovery in the present. Many of the techniques Spencer used in *No Place for an Angel* are present here in a sharper, more succinct narrative. Although only forty-three pages long, "The Cousins" reads more like a novel than a story because of the distances in time and space that it so ably covers. The story closes with the mature "Eric and [Ella Mason] sitting holding hands on a terrace in far-off Italy," and though they are talking in "the pitch black dark," the ending is suffused with a figurative light (72). In retelling their shared past, the two have done Marilee Summerall one better; they have created a common "landscape of the heart" where they may meet again in intimacy. As in "The Business Venture," in "The Cousins" Spencer explores a web of complex and mysterious relationships; however, in "The Cousins," her narrator herself succeeds in healing the wounds of time and distance.

These last four stories suggest at once what Reynolds Price, in reviewing the 1981 collection, called Spencer's "spacious sweep"— the flexibility and range of her mature imagination.[24] Reading Spencer's stories from first to latest reveals her progress: from her early focus on Mississippi to a period of Italian settings and disillusioned, displaced characters; from this focus on displacement and despair to a period of return and reconciliation; and through artistic reconciliation to her final, mature expression. This mature voice exhibits both the distanced objectivity admired by Price—who described Spencer as a "smiling sibyl, unafraid of her news"—and the "power" praised by Eudora Welty (in her foreword to the 1981 volume). Spencer's stories also offer testimony to her growing need to explore more deeply her characters' inner lives, seeking there clues to the nature of intimacy and community. This search led to her technical experimentation of the 1960s and 1970s; often during those years she experimented in the stories with narrative techniques she would later use in the novels. Spencer's artistic "path," her "personal road," has been at times a difficult and frustrating one. Perhaps because of that, her mature work has the depth and richness that results when an artist has shaped out of many and varied fragments a whole vision.

24. Price, "Art of American Short Stories," 20.

8 / Resurrection by Moon and Tide

In many ways, Spencer's first novel after the 1981 collection of stories represents the culmination of her career. *The Salt Line* (1984) is as clearly focused on community as was *The Voice at the Back Door*. In *The Salt Line* Spencer studies the communal healing process that occurs after the kind of loss and destruction suffered by the characters of *No Place for an Angel* and *The Snare*. She also makes extensive use of the mystical elements of human experience, specifically the otherworldly magic she associates with the Gulf coast. The human community of the novel contains several of her typical characters— a female waif, a gangster, an impotent male intellectual, a woman trapped in a restrictive marriage, a stiffly patrician southerner—plus one entirely new figure, an aged Prospero working his caring magic to create a brave new coast.[1]

Although *The Salt Line* has neither the range in time and place of *No Place for an Angel* nor the psychological depth of *The Snare*, it is more concise, more intense, and in many ways a better-made novel than either. In it Spencer weaves together a wide range of characters. While Arnie Carrington acts as a central figure, an aging phallic lightning rod for the novel's action, here, as in much of Spencer's

1. Several commentators have noted the strong echoes of Shakespeare's last play in *The Salt Line*. Rather than seek direct parallels between the two—Evelyn to Ariel or Matteo to Caliban, for example—the more constructive approach is to note the similarities in tone. Like *The Tempest, The Salt Line* is a reconciliation of warring elements, answering destruction and violence with a spiritual acceptance.

early fiction, the concern is with a complex of characters rather than a single human psyche. And unlike in the grey world of Spencer's fiction from the 1960s and 1970s, in which there is figuratively "no place for an angel," in this book there is an angel—a benevolently smiling Buddha sitting in the middle of Arnie Carrington's backyard. The themes of growing acceptance and reconciliation from Spencer's short fiction of the period come to fruition in this novel—one of her two or three finest.

Spencer's central concern in *The Salt Line* is the tidal waxing and waning of successful community in a landscape damaged by a hurricane. She emphasizes the theme of community not with the traditionally melodramatic structure of *The Voice at the Back Door* but with a new structure that is both subtler and more organic to its setting. She uses the novel's four sections to plot alternating low and high tides of communal understanding and acceptance that occur within the larger movement of community recovery. She builds this wavelike pattern of alternating loss and gain out of a number of powerful images, images that finally reveal this tale to be about resurrection on a number of interrelated levels—natural, sexual, and spiritual, as well as communal.

The novel opens on a Gulf coast landscape blasted by Hurricane Camille, which hit in 1969. Natural as well as manmade landmarks have been obliterated. This huge natural disaster mirrors the personal disasters evidenced in the lives of the novel's characters, each of whom has experienced a painful loss.[2] Arnie Carrington's painful sensitivity to the decline of the Gulf coast is exacerbated by the loss of his wife to cancer.[3] Mavis Henley has recently aborted a pregnancy at the suggestion of her lover, Frank Matteo, a charismatic restaurant owner with mob connections. He not only shares this loss with Mavis; he also mourns his own lost childhood and the

---

2. The only exception is the middle-aged mulatto woman Barbra K., who takes a very philosophical attitude toward the shifting fortunes of coastal life. She seems to be the only native of the coast among the novel's main characters.

3. As Prenshaw notes, Phoebe-Lou Adams in her *Atlantic* review argued that "in an oblique way, this is a ghost story, and a very fine one." Prenshaw, *Elizabeth Spencer,* 155; Phoebe-Lou Adams, "Short Reviews," *Atlantic,* CCLIII (February, 1984), 104. Arnie's awareness of Evelyn's ghost is a literal element in the novel, reflective of Spencer's belief that "communication . . . with people who [have] died" is "fairly common." Roberts, "Whole Personality," in *Conversations with Elizabeth Spencer,* ed. Prenshaw, 233.

community acceptance that his reputation denies him. Lex Graham, an academic associate from Arnie's past, has lost any real connection to an emotional present and lives instead a fantasy life with portraits of periwigged eighteenth-century beauties. His wife, Dorothy, is sexually and emotionally starved to the point of desperation, "condemned" to marriage.[4] These are the denizens of a blasted landscape, trying to rebuild their lives as they rebuild the coast.

The "salt line" of the title refers to the point at which, driving south in Mississippi toward the coast, one "can smell the Gulf," where "you could draw the line of that salt smell on the map" (110). The salt line is the border between the "confined and confining" world of rural Mississippi and the magical world of the coast.[5] Each of the novel's main characters comes to the coast to discover "what . . . you did when something's over," how to recover from loss (110). Beyond the salt line, their deepest fears and desires are revealed. Under the influence of a fever brought on by a snakebite, Lex Graham lashes out at his wife and Arnie Carrington, revealing his knowledge of an affair they had had years before. When Dorothy Graham crosses the salt line on the way to nurse the injured Lex, "her blood . . . turned as though the moon had swayed it, and her body, waltzing like underwater seaweed, had begun to know she . . . was going to see [Arnie] again" (103). Mavis Henley's desire to recover Frank Matteo and their lost child leads her inevitably back to his bed; his desire for family, for the intimacy of her conversation, leads him just as inevitably back to her bedside when she bears the resulting child. Arnie Carrington's longing for the coast as he knew it before the hurricane, for the return of his wife, Evelyn, for the resurgence of his sexuality are apparent in his every action.[6] In Spencer's fictional world beyond the salt line, these characters seek recovery and rebirth, rediscovery and resurrection. Those who make accepting, life-affirming decisions find there a new social order, a new family of choice rather than blood, and a new community.

Within this overall movement toward human and social reconstruction, however, Spencer has created two cycles of loss and recov-

4. Elizabeth Spencer, *The Salt Line* (Garden City, N.Y., 1984), 129. Hereinafter cited by page number in the text.

5. Spencer, preface to Spencer, *On the Gulf,* xix.

6. Spencer has said that it was the linguistic connection between the words *resurrection* and *erection* that first led her to think of Arnie's spiritual and emotional loss as compounded by his sexual one.

ery, of human violence and human healing. She draws on the natural rhythms of coastal life—heavily influenced by the rise and fall of the tides and the changing phases of the moon—in designing the structure of *The Salt Line*. Like the tides that are an organic part of coastal life, communal understanding and sympathy in the novel wax and wane. In the novel's opening section (1–51), the community composed of the novel's characters is broken, its members insulated and lonely. In the second part (53–168), there rises a tide of sexual and social rejuvenation that begins to bind them together in a new order. The third part (169–236) chronicles the threats to that new social and familial order, threats that all but destroy it in its infancy. There is a tidal waning of acceptance and understanding that results in senseless violence. Due largely to the caring influence of Arnie *Carring*ton, however, the nascent community survives into the novel's fourth part (237–302), in which a second and higher tide of intimacy rises to form the novel's climax. The function of this ebb and flow is to emphasize that while the novel ends at the point of greatest harmony among its characters, that harmony is both tenuous and fragile. And conversely, because it is so fragile, containing within it the seeds of its own dissolution, that harmony is all the more precious.

Part one, the shortest of the four sections, serves to establish a mood of loss, separation, and despair. The culture that had once existed on the coast has been displaced and largely destroyed. The lives of the characters who have come there are equally fractured and isolated. Arnie is not only angry and dismayed at seeing Lex Graham—they had parted as enemies—he is also deeply in debt as a result of his efforts to save certain coastal properties and in despair over his wife's death. He befriends Mavis Henley primarily because he recognizes in her the same loneliness and disorientation that he feels himself. She has suffered equally as much; Spencer eventually reveals that both have taken the lives of those precious to them, she through abortion and he through an act of euthanasia at his wife's request. For them, as for every other major character in the novel, the universal rule is loneliness. The second chapter makes it clear that even Lex Graham, though accompanied in his new Mercedes by wife and daughter, is as alone and painfully aware of it as any other character in the novel. This opening portrait of despair, however, ends on a positive note that anticipates part two. Intrigued by Mavis' suggestion that he ask Graham, who has just received a large inheritance, for financial backing, Arnie writes to him on impulse, finding in himself both a genuine desire for reunion and some hope for relief.

Part two opens, "When Lex Graham did finally appear to Arnie Carrington, it was after the holidays were done, and a severe freeze had come and gone" (53). Arnie's answer from the "shy, wry, bitter, brilliant Lex" comes after the turn of the year, a change in season that symbolizes the growing possibility for harmony among these disparate characters. Indeed, the novel's second part chronicles both the resurrection of Arnie's sexuality and a growing sense of community among his acquaintances. Although Lex refuses to help Arnie financially, he agrees to spend a day with him on a small island Arnie has bought off the coast as part of his reclamation project. There, Lex is bitten by an unclassified exotic viper or scorpion, and the resulting fever wrings out of him vicious and paranoid fantasies that Arnie and his wife are somehow trying to kill him. Dorothy and Lucinda Graham, his wife and daughter, rush to the coast to help, triggering in the depressed and passive Arnie Carrington an intense response. In the climactic scene of part two, Arnie takes the seventeen-year-old Lucinda Graham to see an old, abandoned lighthouse near the hospital. The girl, acutely aware of Arnie's fame and charisma, is thrilled with the lighthouse's huge, dark echoing interior primarily because of the older man's attention.[7] With him, she "shook herself into place as if grown by an inch: she felt, for the first time, mature" (145).

In turn her freshness and interest in Arnie begin to awaken his dormant sexuality: "The girl . . . was doing the real thing to him, was giving him the good awakening, not the sudden hypodermiclike jolt into lust, but the slow natural freshness, the life of clear water, warm sun, fresh bread. He knew it now: he was going to be all right again. He *knew!*" (144). Once in the lighthouse, he senses her yearning physicality so clearly that "his heart contracted, almost with

---

7. Arnie describes his house to Lucinda while they are in the lighthouse. When he gets to the Buddha, she repeats the word in astonishment. " 'Buddha?' she jumped, spoke louder. ('Oo-dah,' the tower said)" (148). Spencer's use of the echoing lighthouse as the central image within her tidal structure echoes in another sense both the structure and imagery of E. M. Forster's *A Passage to India,* the central image of which is the echoing Marabar cave that frightens Adela Quested. Spencer replaces Forster's nihilistic cave with the bluntly (and comically) phallic lighthouse, and Lucinda Graham, unlike Adela Quested, is thrilled.

pain, before it burst forth, blooming with wonderment. And straight on the heels of that came power, like a flash of fire. The old lighthouse on its green lawn must have teetered from the force of magic within. He called her name, softly, and she turned at once, face flushing with sudden bright expectancy, and in a word, which burst out, . . . she was his, all else thrown aside, claimed forever" (150).

Spencer leaves the extent of their physical intimacy vague, stressing instead the intensity of their mutual admiration. Although she is in her teens and he in his sixties, the power of suddenly awakened, mutual desire unites them. His sexuality resurrected, Arnie hurries to Barbra K., the mulatto shopkeeper who has become his intimate.

Fulfilled and happy after his relationship with Barbra K. is finally consummated, Arnie wanders alone on the beach, thinking happily of Barbra K. "ruffling, furling wavelike over and about him" (167). There he meets Mavis Henley, who has just come from a sexual reunion of her own with Frank Matteo. She is humorously aware of the "coincidence" that "while she was busy with Frank, Arnie had gotten himself going again" (161). Although they are not themselves lovers, the relief of each magnifies that of the other. "The fire that's really lighted will burn forever," is Arnie's comment. "He caught an arm around her bent thigh beside him, and anyone from the highway would have seen them as one shape with two heads against the faded sky" (161).

Together on the beach, they mark the high tide of human sympathy and understanding from the novel's second part. These two, fresh from separate but powerful sexual unions (Mavis is a few hours pregnant), are here figuratively melted into one communal "shape." Walking up to Arnie's house, they see together the Buddha's head floating "free of shadow . . . turned a luminous gray in the moon" (161). The ocean, the beach, and the Buddha radiate peace, but this moment cannot, of course, last; the moon must shift, the tides wane. So Spencer characteristically plants the seeds of disruption and violence in this moment of peace. Later that night, Dorothy Graham slips into Arnie Carrington's house as he sleeps. She enters his bed in despair, coming "not to conquer" in their troubled relationship "but to end it" (168). While their reunion is a fitting coda to this brief season of communion, its despairing, difficult tone signals the season's end.

Earlier in part two, Spencer has used the genesis of a hurricane and the birth of a cancer to dramatize how one season's climax contains within it the seeds of the next:

> In some tiny seeding corner of the Caribbean, a skinny black boy, knife in his teeth, shinnied his way up the long bow-bend of a coconut palm that leaned out over water. A skirl in the tide far out, riding up against a long commalike sand spit, a heat dance of glazed light, and an odd reversal in the wind so that the tree slanted sideways on its lower trunk and a clutch of coconuts, gripped together, drew back from the machete and had to be struck twice over. Only hints of a force that a year later would gather with purpose, like an army for the march.
>
> Maybe right then, or at some other unprovable secret moment like it, deep within Evelyn, one cell was saying an awesome, forbidden word, and another had dreadfully thrilled to hear it, called it to yet another, which had taken it up in turn, until the spread set in like fire, turning life to death, hope to despair. (111–12)

Part three of *The Salt Line* chronicles the waning of intimacy and understanding that naturally follows a high tide of community. In it, Joe Yates, Arnie Carrington's sympathetic business associate, is told what he and the reader had so far only suspected—that Arnie had killed his wife, Evelyn, in an act of loving euthanasia that they had mutually agreed upon. He had buried her on the island they loved and constructed a makeshift shrine over her grave. It becomes obvious at this point that guilt as well as love fuels both Arnie's former impotence and his sensitivity to Evelyn's ghost.

Other ominous events occur. Arnie discovers that Frank Matteo, who has been trying to buy the island from him, is using it to smuggle drugs into the mainland. The Buddha suddenly disappears, taken away by the museum to which its legal owners have relegated it. In an effort to force the city to demolish a storm-wrecked motel he owns, Arnie traps and poisons a colony of rats there. He is sickened by the results. These and other painful events create in Arnie Carrington a growing sense "that distinctions were no longer possible . . . that all of life, good and bad together, was simply one thing" (193).

Spencer weaves into part three of the novel aftereffects of the climaxing "good" from part two: the Grahams' retreat inland, Arnie's relaxed relationship with Barbra K., and his successful revitalizing campaign with Yates (an architect). These all add up to a "common chemistry," with Mavis Henley's pregnancy providing a "kind of musical accompaniment" (195). However, they all sense that their nascent communion is in constant danger during this new season of darkness. Its very existence depends on their not raising any number of threatening issues: "They did not talk about [Barbra K.'s husband] Reuben . . . or about Frank's business being crooked, or about Frank being the father of Mavis's child, or Arnie vanishing in Barbra K.'s direction from time to time, or about Barbra K. being black and the others white. They did not discuss [Joe's wife] Ellen Yates's former drug addiction, though she was still under supervision, or whether Rueben would get it in for Arnie if he found out, or what would happen when the baby came" (196).

Finally, as it had threatened all along, disaster strikes. Arnie had kept in a pond near the Buddha a flock of Oriental ducks, survivors of both the hurricane and scientific research. Nurtured figuratively by the Buddha and literally by the maternal Mavis, they symbolized, for all involved, life at its most innocent and fragile. In the climax of the novel's third part, the cyclical low tide of communal fortunes, the ducks are mysteriously and pointlessly slaughtered. Mavis, already anxious about Matteo's eventual response to her pregnancy, breaks down completely and is only revived by Arnie's sympathy and a day-long boat ride on the tranquil Gulf. Rumors run rampant; it is assumed that a local gang of disaffected youth called the Weasels killed the ducks. The whole community seems suddenly corrupted and in danger of dissolving under the growing pressure. Once Mavis begins to recover, however, Arnie reacts to the threat by sinking into a three-day sleep. Again, Spencer conceals the seeds of the turning tide in the climax, in this instance the low-water mark of the ducks' massacre. After Arnie's symbolic sleep (the death of his despair and uncertainty), he wakes "on the third day, full of sharp certainties, decisive" (235). He will joy in Barbra K., he will protect Mavis Henley as a daughter, and he will sell the island to Matteo. The tide has turned.

At first, the fourth part seems dominated by the death and despair of the third. Its early chapters focus on Lex and Dorothy Graham. He is determined now not to move to the coast, and the psychosis of each feeds on that of the other. Matteo, whose nephew runs with the Weasels, reacts violently to the rumor that they killed the ducks. He burns down the abandoned house in which the gang shelters; one of the group dies in the fire, and the rest scatter. Slowly, however, the tide of kindness and sympathy turns again. Even when angry, Arnie realizes that "it was too late to learn unfeeling ways—for rats or crooks, ducks or waifs or wives" (257). When he visits the Buddha in the museum warehouse, he tells the huge stone idol about his wife's ghost and about the ducks, stopping finally to ask: "How can we gather everything up? Everything we know? Everyone we know? And preferably not as corpses" (277).

Arnie's willingness to accept and forgive, to open himself out into his world, taking in rats as well as ducks, Mafia as well as architects, is the key to the growing sense of community among his friends and acquaintances. Even Frank Matteo catches the communal sensibility, telling Arnie at one point: "The world is one. A nephew is a nephew. Property is property. . . . We are in one world together" (257). As the tide rises, Arnie is reunited with his son. Matteo admits that Mavis' child is his and is slowly drawn into the communal circle, the chosen family of Mavis, Arnie, Barbra K., and the Yateses. But the destructive, life-denying force has one last blow to strike in *The Salt Line*. Lex Graham, his wife institutionalized, wanders periodically back to the coast in search of peace. When Mavis is seven months into her pregnancy, he enters her shop one day to deliver a rambling, psychotic monologue, admitting in passing that he butchered the ducks. The shock sends her into labor, and all concerned converge on the Notchaki Hospital.

In the back of the careening ambulance with the hemorrhaging Mavis, Arnie "prayed to God, to Buddha, to whatever there was, to the power within." Barbra K., holding Mavis' other hand, "call[ed] on Jesus." "It was hope," Spencer writes, "that they were riding with, swift as a charged cloud, ready to gather strength and speed, to break with hurricane force into the bright redemption of love" (298). In this and the concluding pages that follow, Spencer adopts a powerfully lyrical tone, choosing diction that creates out of the child's birth a storm force of love and hope, the human community's answer to the storms that had all but destroyed their lives. The child struggling to be born, "a life on its thundering way to light," is the product of their communal love and bears all their hope. Arnie even recruits the skeptical Yates to find and bring Matteo to the hospital. Arnie sits in the waiting room, "knowing the strain of what the keystone of the world's arch knows constantly—that everything has only the one chance in infinity of going right, but those there are who are always taking it" (299). At the news that both Mavis and her premature son are all right, Arnie collapses.

Significantly, it is Matteo who pulls him up and supports him. "This damned crook," Arnie thinks of Matteo, "this dark projection in [our] lives" (301–302), who even at this strained moment does not fully trust the others.[8] Had they "trapped" him into their circle of dependency and love? Matteo could not know and is defiant while becoming, almost despite himself, one of them. " 'You think that [seeing my son]'s not all there is,' he challenged. 'You think for a minute that's not all?' " (302). At that moment, the last in the novel, the newborn *is* all there is for any of them. What had begun in shared destruction and death ends in shared birth.

In the magical realm of the Gulf coast, where time is measured by the changing moon and shifting tides, Spencer has studied in detail the organic growth of a human community. The circle of human salvage that she collects in the Notchaki Hospital maternity ward has triumphed over the forces that would fracture and disperse them. The common element that links them together is the genially accepting, life-affirming presence of Arnie Carrington. He represents one of the two conflicting forces that generate the continual tension in the novel. His is the power of the life force: romantic (a Byron scholar); young ("I was never any age but yours," he tells Lucinda Graham); and, once he is rejuvenated, powerfully phallic.[9] The lesson he teaches those he loves is the lesson of rebirth, rediscovery, and resurrection. He answers with his life the question "What do you do when something ends?" He answers it simply by, as Mavis puts it, "tak[ing] things and go[ing] on" (292). He *cares* in a profoundly patient, profoundly self-effacing way, and his caring makes a supreme difference in each life he touches.

The force that opposes him in *The Salt Line* is centered in his

8. The mood of this section echoes the closing scenes of *The Tempest,* in which Prospero forgives his enemies and remarks of Caliban, who had tried to murder him and rape his daughter, "This thing of darkness I acknowledge mine" (V, i, 275–76).

9. Spencer hints that Arnie has a power almost beyond that of normal humans. His charisma plus her emphasis on his phallic rejuvenation suggest a number of ancient fertility myths, particularly that of Osiris. The ancient Egyptians believed that the fertility of the land was tied directly to the annual phallic resurrection of the god Osiris, and the ceremony in which the god's powers were invoked involved "the dispatch of geese to the four points of the compass" to announce the turning season and "the king and queen . . . [having] intercourse." H. W. Fairman, "The Kingship Rituals of Egypt," in *Myth, Ritual, and Kingship,* ed. S. H. Hooke (Oxford, England, 1958), 85.

onetime friend and colleague Lex Graham. Graham's is the power of distance, of insulation, and of death: neoclassical (he lusts after reproductions of eighteenth-century Lucindas), aged beyond his years ("poor old Lex" is his refrain), and chronically dysfunctional. "Sexual despair is not my affair," he puns to himself in a memo on his wife's illness (106). He constantly seeks distance, not only from his wife, but from any flesh-and-blood being except his daughter, whom he tries to make over in the image of his pure eighteenth-century virgins. He is a killer both of the spirit (Dorothy's primarily) and of the flesh. It is only after he rejects the coast as a place to live that a community begins to form around Carrington.

These two forces—phallic and life-affirming versus bitter and life-denying—are at war in the novel's blasted landscape, and the characters' lives are shaped by which of the two they follow. Dorothy Graham, for example, is trapped in her cold, unfulfilling marriage and lacks the will to divorce her husband and his newfound wealth. Even her love for Arnie is not enough to break her free of Lex's chilling influence. Her decision to stay with him is life-denying, even life-threatening. At novel's end, she faces life in a series of institutions where she will be treated for alcoholism and sexual addiction. Her fate serves as a constant reminder that though it ends happily, *The Salt Line* is not a sentimental tale, and those characters who follow Arnie Carrington must earn their limited victories. Mavis Henley chooses to continue after suffering through a violently failed marriage, a stalled relationship with Matteo, and an abortion. Matteo's body, though beautiful, is as scarred as his psyche, and though he could never admit it, Arnie knows that the abortion has devastated him. He loses face as well as syndicate money in his dealings with Arnie and Yates and yet decides to accept their aid and offer his own at the end. Arnie's son, angered and confused by the death of his stepmother, also finally chooses to accept his father. Arnie's romantic spirit even seduces Yates, the eminently practical architect, and they slave together on Arnie's obviously nonremunerative schemes. Finally, there is Barbra K., Arnie's spiritual sister and lover; at the climax of the novel, as they sit in the maternity ward waiting room, Arnie realizes suddenly that "she looked like Evelyn." She has "the same amplitude. Arnie had never noticed it so strongly as now. When had he first seen it? Perhaps down where nothing got actually told, down where the knowing started, beyond where the words began and ended. We can go to the island one day, he thought, surprising himself. But no need to go there, really, with her here, ashore" (301).

Through Barbra K.—black, married, maternal—Arnie has found not only himself reerected but also the spirit of his dead wife. And through Barbra K. even Evelyn's spirit is present for Arnie at the birth that ends the novel. The island—symbolic of his insulation, his desperate hold on the past—is no longer necessary to Arnie. He has found a new family in those who have chosen him as father, friend, or lover.

The fragile circle of support and love formed by these characters is, in contrast to Spencer's protagonists of the 1960s and 1970s, the central concern of the novel. *The Salt Line* is, to borrow Hubert Creekmore's description of *Fire in the Morning,* "a study . . . of the character of a complex of people" as that complex is forming.[10] Although the narrative point of view is not as important in conveying this theme as the structure, the ways in which Spencer manipulates her omniscient point of view contributes to the theme of community.

The figure of Arnie Carrington is central to the novel's development, but Spencer does not associate the narrative point of view primarily with him, as she tended to do with her protagonists in *Knights and Dragons* and *The Snare.* Instead she moves the point of view into and out of the minds of a number of characters—notably Lex Graham, Frank Matteo, Dorothy Graham, and Mavis Henley, as well as Arnie Carrington. In chapter six of part one, for example, Spencer follows Carrington closely during a night of soul-searching, slipping adeptly in and out of his first-person reflections and capturing whole passages of interior monologue while still nominally in a third-person voice. In chapter two of part two she uses the same techniques to enter the personality of Graham. In chapter eight of part three she portrays Frank Matteo's past through Mavis Henley's loving recollections of their pillow talk. Their intimacy fuels both her desire to understand and his desire to be understood. In the last part of the novel (specifically chapter nine), Mavis is exhausted by her pregnancy and often sits drifting in and out of sleep, dreaming on the edge of consciousness of things real and unreal. Spencer ranges through the free-flowing stream of Mavis' consciousness, her waking and dreaming monologue, and blends the remembered past

10. Creekmore, "Submerged Antagonisms," 16.

into the actual present. The result of Spencer's subtly shifting point of view in these and other scenes is that the community consciousness becomes the organic material for the novel.

If the first distinctive thing about this community's history is its tidal structure, the second is the powerful images that propel it forward. In the summer of 1990, Spencer described how the novel developed in "its own, unexpected way." She recalled: "I had whole blocks of *The Salt Line* that I had to throw away because they didn't pertain to the central images in the book. Those images I think are what control that novel. If I tried while writing that book to follow the narrative line and left the images, it just wouldn't work. But when I stuck to the central vision, things just flowed."[11]

The landmark images that Spencer refers to are the Buddha, the ducks that flock around it, Lex Graham's Mercedes and his collection of prints, Arnie Carrington's three pieces of property, and, most powerful of all, the cluster of phallic symbols, including the water tower and the lighthouse. These images impel the novel's development and reveal the secret natures of its characters.

Spencer associates the statue of the Buddha, parked by Camille in Arnie Carrington's backyard, with Carrington. The patient acceptance of adversity that it implies becomes part and parcel of his personality as he grows into a life without Evelyn. When Dorothy Graham travels to the coast in response to Lex's illness, she discovers in the hospital waiting room a dozing Arnie, unkempt and aged, and she recognizes that "something new had come to him, and . . . worst of all, that it was good. It spoke to her out of the quality of his patience. It . . . led her nowhere but to goodness of the humane sort, asking more about need itself than whose need, about what, more than who" (104).

As Arnie's growing patience and his innate ability for caring begin to attract a potential community, all who know him come to share his accepting attitude. Or as Spencer described it in an interview, the Buddha "came to mean for me the possible harmony, the harmonious qualities of the East which didn't exist between these characters until after the irritants, namely Lex and his wife, are gradually thrown aside, and the harmonies return between people."[12] Even after the

11. Roberts, "Whole Personality," in *Conversations with Elizabeth Spencer*, ed. Prenshaw, 222–23.

12. *Ibid.*, 219–20.

Buddha's removal to the museum, its influence continues to grow with the group through Arnie's presence.

At the foot of the statue in Arnie's yard shelter the incongruous flock of Oriental ducks. Silly and loud, they are devoted to only two beings: Mavis Henley, who feeds them, and the Buddha, who watches over them. They seem at first a misplaced and inconsequential landmark. Appropriately, they represent a complementary element to the Buddha's implacable spirituality. They are loud, brazen, opinionated, and, in their physicality, tragically vulnerable. They represent the dependence and fragility present in each of the novel's characters and, as a flock, the nascent community of those characters. Thus it is the waif Mavis who is most sensitive to their needs. Their death in part three represents the lowest, most threatening point in the community's life. Arnie, Mavis, Yates, and even Matteo are deeply wounded, as the loss of the ducks touches each at his or her most vulnerable point.

The man who destroys the ducks and who directly or indirectly threatens each of the novel's other characters has his own cluster of identifying images. Lex Graham appears so consistently in his new beige Mercedes, self-assured in its richly air-conditioned status, that it becomes an inseparable part of his persona. The car is symbolic of his obsession with possessions—"Chinese porcelains, English prints, framed portraits of eighteenth century ladies . . . new dinner service . . . impeccable"—all of which serve to insulate him from his life's emptiness and failure (293). His sole sexual impulse is fueled by his reproductions of portraits of eighteenth-century ladies, "flounces and ribbons and platinum perukes and little curls and beauty spots and powder" (32). Bitter, insecure, and paranoid, he rejects any opportunity for emotional healing and communal acceptance when he lashes out against Arnie Carrington and the coast. All of his neoclassical possessions fail him because he uses them to isolate himself from the human community rather than to connect with it. He treats his wife and daughter as possessions to be cultivated in the same way as these artifacts, forcing their ultimate reaction against him. Lex Graham's relationship to his treasured possessions does not change during the course of the novel because his is a static, dead personality.

His perceived opponent, Arnie Carrington, also has a cluster of possessions that define him, but unlike Graham, his relationship to these properties changes as he develops. Carrington has bought three pieces of property as part of his reclamation project: the island where he buried his wife, the wrecked Hotel Miramar, and a group of rundown row houses that he plans to convert into shops.[13] He struggles financially to hang on to the island through the first half of the novel just as he struggles to hang on to his dead wife. Significantly, he decides to sell it to Matteo precisely at the end of part three, when he turns away from his past and toward the future. His decision to sell marks both his inspired acceptance of Matteo and his own newly discovered emotional freedom. It is a life-affirming decision, as is that to raze the wrecked hotel. The Miramar is an old, elegant, rambling structure that had before Camille captured the essence of the coast's culture. Carrington's decision to have it torn down and the property developed comes at a key moment in the development of his nature and his new community. His sexual resurrection at the end of part two frees him of his obsession with the past and enables him to act decisively to move forward.

Spencer dramatizes this forward movement with Arnie's development of the row houses into a series of small businesses and shops. The significant others of his new family relocate there: Mavis' art shop and students, Barbra K.'s day-care center, and Yates's architectural office. This property, unlike the other two, has a future; it physically joins those who had before led lonely, isolated lives. It becomes a symbol of what Arnie's caring perseverance and attention to human life have accomplished. These three "properties" are, of course, properties of Arnie's character as well as his mortgage listing. The island suggests his solitariness and his guilty obsession with his wife's death. The Miramar "mirrors" his sensitivity to a lost culture, a way of life swept away by time and weather. The row houses, the most mundane of all, represent his willingness to forgo the past and enter the future, building a new community and a new family on the ruins of the old.

Spencer portrays the power that enables him to wreak this change as blatantly, even comically phallic. The university water tower that Arnie climbs after a campus protest is the first example of this phallic motif. As he climbs it out of sheer spontaneous exuberance, Lex Graham sights down a pistol barrel at him from a distance, thinking

---

13. Spencer also contrasts Arnie's house with Graham's. Rather than expensive antiques and tasteful artifacts, he has furnished his unobtrusive refuge with the salvage that survived the hurricane, suggesting once again his concern for caring conservation as opposed to Lex's status-starved acquisition.

no one sees him. Spencer contrasts Arnie's glorious and quite phallic charisma with Lex's impotent inability to fire his pistol. In this same phallic motif, Spencer strikes a number of minor notes: "Lucinda with her little unicorn's horn of blessing" (102), the writhing snakes on the belt Arnie is wearing when his vitality returns, and Frank Matteo's masculine appearance as "a tower looking down" (131). The center piece in this cluster of images, however, is the lighthouse where Arnie is magically brought to rebirth by the virginal Lucinda. The lighthouse functions not only as the site of an all-but-mythical sexual rebirth; it is also appropriate to Spencer's purposes because it is a coastal beacon. The rejuvenation of Arnie's ability to love— metaphysical as well as physical—will inspire all those he is gathering around him. It is no accident in Spencer's design that at that moment, Mavis Henley and Frank Matteo are physically reunited and their son conceived. The lighthouse is the phallic beacon that will lead these fragmented characters back into a communal circle.

The Salt Line is, in a sense, a reply to Spencer's novels of the 1960s and 1970s. In it Spencer takes as her subject as broad a spectrum as No Place for an Angel but to very different ends. She asks again the question of both Knights and Dragons and The Snare—"What do you do when something ends?"—and answers it in a new and profoundly spiritual way. In this fine novel Spencer, through the magic of tides and moonlight beyond the salt line, resolves the sense of disunity and loss that had haunted her three previous novels.

9 / *The Ties That Bind Are Holding Forever*

The Night Travellers (1991), Elizabeth Spencer's ninth novel, contrasts starkly with *The Salt Line*, published seven years before. Whereas *The Salt Line* is drenched with sunlight and salt water, *The Night Travellers* is shrouded in darkness and snow. Whereas *The Salt Line* chronicles the resurrection of lost communion among its characters, *The Night Travellers* portrays separation and destruction. Despite these and other differences, *The Night Travellers* bears the earmarks of Spencer's best fiction—technical experimentation and focus on community.

In the tradition of *No Place for an Angel*, *The Night Travellers* examines in detail a period in American cultural history. Set in the 1960s, it portrays America under the shadow of the Vietnam War and the counterculture that grew up in opposition to the war. Spencer has carefully chosen her characters to reveal the intense, often violent pressures affecting American community and family life during the period. At one point in the novel, she even writes of two central characters, a mother and her small daughter, that though "they gave off an aspect of stillness, like the surface of a pool . . . back of that stillness all the wretched turmoil of a decade" lay hidden. These and other characters are "like a keyhole to look through," Spencer writes, "or a special lens."[1] By focusing her readers' attention through the

1. Elizabeth Spencer, *The Night Travellers* (New York, 1991), 321. Hereinafter cited by page number in the text.

"lens" of these particular characters—a weapons researcher and her daughter, the antiwar activist her daughter marries, and others—Spencer emphasizes once again how intricately interwoven are public and private lives. "The world is linked," as one character tells another, "bound together" in a web of inescapable relationships (323). And though the political and generational conflict of the 1960s stretched many intimate relationships to the breaking point and beyond, these characters constantly strive to nurture and be nurtured by one another, to maintain the vital contacts even across time and distance.

To dramatize the conflict and alienation of the 1960s, Spencer uses not only a wide range of settings and characters but also multiple narrators in a variety of narrative forms. She includes long passages from a minor character's journal, transcripts of audio recordings, letters as read both by the woman to whom they were written and by another who intercepts and destroys them, and dramatized chapters of apparently disembodied voices. Spencer uses all of these nominally first-person forms, "written" or "spoken" by various characters, in addition to the roving perspective of her omniscient viewpoint. The result is a complex community of perspectives that emphasizes structurally the theme of the novel, that individual human beings are defined by their relations to others, even when physically removed from those they love.

To structure her study of community dynamics in *The Night Travellers*, Spencer returned to the ebb and flow of community that she created in *The Salt Line*. The titles of the five parts of *The Night Travellers* are obvious clues to this pattern. Part one, "The Home Scene," describes Mary's childhood with emphasis on the death of her father and her mother's abusive nature. Spencer opens part two, "Voices from Afar," with Gerda Stewart's journal and moves the action forward through a variety of narrative "voices" already mentioned. In terms of both the narrative structure and the plot, part two portrays the dissolution of the traditional American community and family. In part three, aptly named "Scatterings," the fragments of the original human community drift farther apart, and Mary's state of mind reaches what is, except for her suicide attempt, its lowest point.

But in part four, "Reunion," the tide turns. Jeff, traveling in disguise, manages to reach Montreal and is reunited with Mary and Kathy. This is the high tide of communion, toward which these characters have struggled since early in the novel. Their fellow feeling and common need are so intense that Jeff decides to turn himself in to face legal consequences so that later they can all live together in peace. In part five, "Divisions and Dilemmas," he is drafted and ̣s last seen caught in a hellish firefight in the Vietnamese jungle. As the novel ends, he has a vision of Mary approaching him yet again through the trees as she had so many years before in North Carolina. It is an ominous but not necessarily tragic ending.

Within this larger structure, Spencer deftly portrays layer upon layer of significant relationships. Within the larger web of the novel's characters, however, exist three important patterns, groups of closely related characters that are a part of the novel's unifying structure. Each of the three groups forms a significant pattern, the relationships of which shape the characters' lives.

The first of these patterns is the direct maternal lineage that ties mother to daughter to granddaughter. The mother, Kate Harbison, is a socially ambitious, Duke University–trained scientist who, though beautiful and intelligent, is quite unstable. "Lyrically lovely, with the efficiency record of an M1 rifle," she often physically and verbally abuses her young daughter, Mary Kerr Harbison, particularly after the death of the girl's father (85). Kate's world is defined by her lab research, which involves testing chemical weapons on animals for the military, and the country club. Her daughter, on the other hand, is from early childhood passionately interested in dance. Unlike her mother, she cares little for social distinctions and falls in love with Jefferson Blaise, an idealistic and gifted young war protester whose name recalls Thomas Jefferson, one of America's foremost advocates of revolution, and hints at the violence of the 1960s.

The conflict between mother and daughter is almost primal, having sprung from their earliest competition for the affection of Mary's father. "Poppy loved me," Mary often thought. "You're always mad because he loved me. If you don't love me, why can't you let me go?" (29). Even at their most cordial, mother and daughter live in fundamental discord, a fact that becomes all the more obvious after the birth of Mary's own daughter, Kathy, whom, ironically, she names after her mother. Together, the three form a profoundly significant "line of three women" bound together by genetics and love but unable to live together (195). Spencer makes it clear that they are torn apart not just by the societal conflicts of the times but also by Kate's perversity. Kate Harbison is congenitally unresponsive to the affection offered first by her daughter and later by her grand-daughter. She is cold, cunning, and efficient, both as scientist and social climber, but she does not have the emotional capacity to honor the ties of love that bind her to others.

Kate's lack of respect for her daughter becomes painfully obvious in the second primal set of relationships that link the two. When Kate first meets Jeff Blaise, she is both deeply disturbed by and strongly attracted to him. Her reaction is so intensely sexual that she wonders "if Mary Kerr would know what to do with him" (49) and, in a chapter Spencer entitles "The Triangle," invites him to meet her privately. Without admitting her motives even to herself, she approaches him suggestively: "Her white hand came up and rested on his shoulder. The ground might as well have rippled like a snake on the move. What she was saying might be one thing, but what was she meaning to do here—" (70–71). Jeff is immediately aware of the moment's sexual overtones and accuses her of trying to seduce him to destroy his relationship with Mary. From that moment his involvement with Kate is nearly as complex as that with Mary. Kate had, he thought, "one way or another . . . thrown a noose around him" (71). He goes immediately to Mary and, partially titillated by his encounter with her mother, makes love to her in an empty dance studio. Ironically, it is at this moment, when both are haunted by Kate, that they realize they have "a chance at forever" (72). As a result, their partnership exists always in the context of Kate. Kate in turn is so obsessed by Jeff that she will later try again to seduce him, read and destroy letters he has written to Mary, and even ask her wealthy second husband to have Jeff "blotted out some way" (195). Mary knows or suspects all of this and realizes just how intensely she must compete with her mother even in her own courtship and marriage.

Mary combats Kate and any other forces that would permanently separate her from Jeff with her own abiding vision of their relationship. After a suicide attempt in Canada, she records on the audio tape provided by her psychiatrist when and where she first encountered this vision. It had begun, she tells the tape recorder, "because of a picture I had once long ago." She continues:

It had grown on me, become like a vision, not to be lost. It was a picture in one of Mother's science texts at home in Kingsbury. A group, a family, imagined as having lived long before any history began to be written down or even remembered. Three were in it: a mother seated by the fire, the child on her lap, the father just standing from having built up the fire, just turning from looking out into the dark to reassure their safety, just about to turn back to them. . . . While Jeff was there . . . I would think, *This is the way we feel about ourselves, the three of us, the way it has been and will be.* (151)

Like the matriarchal lineage and the competitive triangle, this pattern—mother, child, and father united against the threatening world—takes on primal power during the course of the novel. When Canadian authorities take Kathy away from Mary after her suicide attempt, she struggles to regain her identity, realizing, as she puts it, that "when Kathy gets returned to me, I will know I'm real, and so will everything else be" (157). She derives her identity, even her sense of reality, from her vision of herself as wife and mother. Her original nuclear family had been destroyed by her father's death, and her own marriage is threatened by Jeff's lengthy absences. And yet she is able to retain her faith in him, survive as a single mother in an alien country, and inspire his continued activities through the power of her vision.

By structuring the novel with these patterned groups, Spencer emphasizes their significance in human life. She makes it clear that the relationships contained in these groups—parent and child, wife and husband, lover and lover—are the primary source of human identity. With the exception of those relationships tainted by Kate Harbison's instability, all these bonds are ultimately nurturing, even under the worst possible conditions. In fact, their impact on individual identity is so pervasive that the only escape from their influence is through death. When early in the novel Jeff asks Mary to abandon her mother and her mother's life-style, she replies: "I can't do it even if I do it. Dying is the only leaving" (67). Alone and desperate in Canada, Mary tries to kill herself, rationalizing the attempt not out of her own pain but out of a desire simply to "vanish" out of the pattern of others' lives, "to get out of the way" (150, 191). And when Kate's obsession with Jeff becomes too pervasive to bear, she asks her husband to have him "blotted out some way. [She] didn't say dead exactly," but of course that is what she means, as she, too, realizes that death is the only way to remove yourself or another from the human community (195).

Family relationships as Spencer portrays them are so fundamental to human identity that all the characters in the novel except Kate and her second husband, Fred Davis, honor them instinctively. In a world where traditional communities have been shattered by social strife, social and cultural refugees must find "family" where they can. The Montreal of the 1960s, as Spencer pictures it, is home to count-less numbers of those the world has rejected: draft evaders and war protesters, European Jews and homosexual artists, all emotional gyp-sies seeking a home. All the novel's major characters, whether in Canada or the States, are seeking to replace those key relationships that have somehow been lost. Both Mary and Jeff seek a father and find one for a while in Ethan Marbell, Jeff's academic mentor. During Jeff's absence, Mary seeks a family for Kathy and forms a makeshift household with her homosexual dance partner, Estes Drover. During her father's absence, the toddler Kathy draws emotional substance from a series of good men: the Canadian hunter Monsieur Gerard as well as Estes Drover, whose violent arguments with his lover she blithely ignores. Even the icy, manipulative Kate senses an emptiness in her life; having lost Mary, she hopes to use Kathy to prove herself as a mother. In stressing their efforts to replace lost loved ones, Spencer highlights just how primal these relationships are.[2] Without them, the characters themselves do not fully exist. They are defined by those they love, whether that love is successfully expressed or not.

Ironically, Jeff and Mary Blaise's marriage is the most successful relationship in the novel, and yet circumstance forces them apart. Spencer's title, *The Night Travellers*, refers indirectly to the world of midnight border crossings and shrouded subterfuge in which they live. The nuclear family formed by Jeff, Mary, and Kathy Blaise is threatened from its very genesis by Jeff's opposition—on grounds of conscience—to the war; he spends most of the novel "underground" in the States, leaving Mary and Kathy alone in Canada. After Mary's suicide attempt, the nucleus is split even farther apart when the Canadian courts send Kathy to live with Kate and Fred. Although Jeff and Mary love each other faithfully and long to live together, this small unit of human caring is ripped apart by social conflict, most

2. When Jeff Blaise is forced to hide for a time with a group of San Francisco reactionaries who have turned insanely violent, he encounters an ironic reversal of the need for family. A Georgia country boy on the run from the draft drifts into the group and is tortured and finally beaten to death for his refusal to renounce his family. Humanity is defined, Spencer argues, by its need for the nurturing intimacy of community, most fundamentally by its need for family. Meaningless brutality results when that need is denied.

of which is not of their own making.[3] The novel's central irony is that those who have access to their families fail to appreciate them while those, like Mary and Jeff, who appreciate each other are tragically separated. They and many of their brethren in the movement are the disinherited, the travellers by night to whom Spencer refers in her title. When Jeff and the pregnant Mary first slip across the border into Canada, they are entering an alien environment, banished by their beliefs from their own country. Several months after her suicide attempt, loneliness compels Mary to slip back across the border to steal Kathy back from Kate. Throughout this agonizing time, her communications with Jeff are few and far between, their letters—many of his containing money—lost or stolen by movement couriers. They are, as Jeff suggests, like underground soldiers in a second great Civil War, and Spencer associates the imagery of darkness and of the night with them from early in the novel.

First Jeff and later Mary become members of the 1960s counterculture, the flip side of the "straight" culture and reminiscent of Julia Garrett's "crooked" world in *The Snare*. The obvious difference is that this counterworld is based on its own idealistic vision, a moral straightness of intent. Despite this, however, Spencer describes this world with images of the darkness suggested in the title. Early in the novel, Mary thinks of Jeff as having come from "the night," and as "slipping [back] into bayou-dark water, a night-bird careening off into the shadows" (50). She fears him and wants to "let him go, back into the dark with all his darkness" (53). She cannot, however, resist his allure, the romantic tie that binds her to him almost against her will, and she, too, comes to be associated with darkness, thinking that "somewhere through the blackness, there must be a landing place . . . for her" (115). Their lives together lead them to one "dangerous border" after another—"Night crossings. Regroupings" (175). They become "children of the dark," their very survival dependent on secrecy and disguise (200). And yet their public and private trials strengthen them, so that eventually both Jeff and Mary come to value their life *together* more than any social or political issue.

3. That Jeff and Mary's marriage is "faithful" is not in doubt despite a single episode of sexual indiscretion on the part of each. Their desperation for affection in a Canada that is both literally and figuratively frigid accounts for their brief infidelities, and Spencer obviously intends both to become more human and more sympathetic in the reader's eyes.

Their final, mutual decision to reunite at all costs is significant because it resolves, for them at least, the novel's central conflict— that between political or public conscience and private desire. This novel, like the earlier *Voice at the Back Door*, has as a primary theme the indissoluble ties between public and private life. In the politically charged world of *The Night Travellers*, there is no public action without private consequences and no private decision without political or social implications. Spencer uses irony to emphasize this idea through Mary Harbison, who is swept into the center of the antiwar movement by her relationship with Jeff despite her almost total political apathy. In turn, Jeff's commitment to a political course that values individual rights denies him a significant private life. From the other end of the spectrum, Kate's deft management of her various courtships after the death of her first husband is blatantly political; she sifts through various admirers, probing delicately for evidence of wealth and influence, until she discovers Fred Davis' Main Line riches. Fred Davis manipulates his political and financial contacts to have Jeff Blaise hounded and eventually sent to Vietnam to be "blotted out" of his wife's mind (195). No character is exempt; those from both sides of the political fence are caught up in the social and political web of their culture. So tightly are their private lives bound by their public ones that in order to live a normal life with his family, Jeff must turn himself in to American authorities and be drafted into active service, unknowingly submitting himself to a fate orchestrated by Fred Davis. In making this decision, Jeff and Mary are gambling with his life, illustrating clearly both the stress they are under and the intensity of their desire to live together at all costs.

In the turbulent world of Spencer's 1960s, however, public strife has stretched the private ties that bind individuals almost to the breaking point. Spencer uses a variety of narrative strategies to dramatize the alienation and disorientation that results. From the beginning of the novel's second section, she weaves five different first-person forms into her largely omniscient narrative: passages from the journal of Gerda Stewart, a conservative, middle-class Canadian; the text of Mary's audio recordings of her own jumbled memories and emotions; Jeff's letters, often mysteriously coded, often interrupted; his "lost" letters, collected by Ethan Marbell and read by Mary in one agonizing sitting; and four chapters of disembodied dramatic dialogue. These "voices" serve to dramatize the theme of separation and alienation in two ways. First, each of the forms is in itself indicative of the characters' refugee status. Even Gerda Stewart's journal is the result of her own middle-aged loneliness and alienation from her husband. Second, together they create the sense that the novel itself is made up of isolated voices crying out for human contact and warmth. Out of enforced isolation of every sort, these characters use language to try desperately to maintain human contact.

After 115 pages of omniscient narration, Spencer opens the second part of *The Night Travellers*, "Voices from Afar," with two chapters from Gerda Stewart's journal. Spencer uses the journal of this middle-aged Montreal housewife to dramatize the loneliness and disconnection suffered by all in this time and place. Gerda is married to Mary's affluent landlord, Gordon Stewart. Because of Gordon's kindly interest in Mary, she becomes involved with the Blaises, and it is through her oblique point of view that Spencer relates Mary's lonely suicide attempt. In these and succeeding journal entries, Gerda emerges as a lonely woman who takes up the journal as one in a series of hobbies to fill the midlife void left by distant children and a vague, absentminded husband. Her growing interest in Mary and Jeff becomes all but an obsession as her fear that Gordon has fallen in love with Mary grows. When Jeff passes unannounced through Montreal looking for Mary, only Gerda Stewart sees his lonely, silent figure. "We're her friends," she tells him urgently, but he utters only one word—"Impossible"—and walks away (129). His despairing, existential outcry stands as a comment on the entire confused situation. Although Gerda has, as she admits, a "conservative soul," both she and her "poor Gordon with his limp" live vicariously for a while through Jeff and Mary. Eventually the Stewarts withdraw into their lonely, grey lives, unable to understand the Blaises' lack of respect for property and status. Spencer's point is made; Gerda's reflections are in the form of a journal because she has no one with whom she can share them. As both the form and content of her message make clear, she has no nurturing and vital connection.

In the same way, Mary's tape-recorded meditations are tinged with desperation. When she does not respond to her state-appointed counselor, the "lady psychiatrist" gives her a tape recorder so she can talk out her frustrations in private (158). Mary uses the tapes to create her own private version of her life, which only the reader has access to. Spencer stands behind Mary using her tape-recorded musings to stress just how fundamentally disturbing is her isolation. Beginning in chapter three of the novel's second part, these taped meditations make up eleven chapters, revealing in Mary a restless, nervy intellect and a strong sense of her own role and purpose. Her confession that she tried to kill herself in order to "vanish" out of the family web is both frightening and enlightening (150). Left "alone a lot" by Jeff and abandoned by their "gypsying friends," she thinks that if she could only disappear, then Kathy could return to Aunt Jane's money and Aunt Sally's "bootees, little knitted sweaters, funny embroidered romp suits" (150). Her attempt to disappear is genuine and desperate, the result of a loneliness so compelling, an existential isolation so destructive, that to Mary "all became like dream objects and motions like in a dream, moving in the current with a dreamy rhythm" (151). In the aftermath of her suicide attempt, she rediscovers her identity when she remembers all the people who were "real" to her emotionally: "When Kathy gets returned to me, I will know I'm real, and so will everything else be. I want her back. I want to carry her like a kangaroo mother carries her baby, in a pouch, while leaping yards at a jump, through the snow. . . . It's breaking up now, melting and getting filthy dirty, trying to hold on, but fading. It's going. Dying is going. It didn't work" (157).

By couching Mary's recovery in her own words, Spencer is able to stress how fundamentally contextual is her identity. The tone, the diction, and the pacing of what Mary says into her tape recorder rise optimistically and fall despondently in direct relation to her contact with those who are real to her, those to whom she is vitally connected.

That the recordings are necessary at all is the explicit result of her suicide attempt, but at a deeper level they are the result of the loss of identity that in Spencer's world results from isolation. Like Martha Ingram in *Knights and Dragons*, Mary Blaise discovers that severing even the constrictive ties that bind can have emotionally disastrous consequences. Unlike Martha Ingram, however, Mary rebounds through her successful ties to husband, child, and friends. In Mary's recordings, Spencer found a medium perfectly reflective of her situation. Unable to talk to anyone else, Mary Blaise talks to herself.

In the same sense, Jeff's series of letters to her—often interrupted, often coded, almost always pilfered for money—dramatize the political threats to their relationship. Spencer emphasizes that theirs is a dysfunctional culture, one in which a successful marriage is all but impossible. While Mary is pregnant with Kathy, Jeff has a brief affair with an older Canadian woman.⁴ This brief indulgence of his loneliness costs both him and Mary dearly. After Jeff leaves to rejoin the movement in America, Mary finds a passionate letter to him from his lover. Partly because of the timing involved—they would not see each other for months—this incident nearly destroys them. Mary's suicide attempt, she tells Ethan Marbell, was largely the result of her sense that Jeff was "gone for good" (248). In turn, the rumors of her near death drive him nearly wild with anguish. And yet, in a pattern reminiscent of the tidal structure Spencer used in *The Salt Line*, the couple's mutual faith slowly returns. When Ethan Marbell eventually finds Mary in the wilds of Ottawa, where she has gone to hide, he brings a bundle of Jeff's letters scavenged from across the States. Although they had been written over months of desperate activity and furtive hiding, she reads them all during one long night.

The record of Jeff and Mary's all-but-aborted correspondence is a telling commentary on the nature of their society. Spencer makes it clear that because of their alienation from community, family, and country, the bond that joins them is stretched to its limit.⁵ They cannot resolve the emotional aftereffects of Jeff's affair simply because it is almost impossible for them to contact each other. The first letter brought to Mary by Ethan is postmarked "somewhere near SF" (Jeff cannot be more explicit for fear of FBI interception) and opens, "It's no better for you than thinking you're married to some guy in jail to think of me, I know" (249). His analogy is particularly apt except that their enforced separation is largely a result of conscious choices they both have made—to oppose the war, to live in Canada, to have Kathy. Bound by these mutual decisions, they fight on in isolation to preserve their mutuality, the first of Spencer's major characters to face this peculiarly Spencerian dilemma.

In the dark Canadian wintertime, Mary is forced to subsist on

4. Spencer adds the voice of Jeff's lover, Madeleine Spivak, to the chorus of the disaffected. In chapter nineteen of part two, entitled "The Torch Song of Madeleine Spivak (Love Does Not Grow Old)," she mourns Jeff's loss.

5. Because of Spencer's emphasis on the failure of the family (and other groups), the most disturbing misplacement of all Mary and Jeff's correspondence occurs when Ethan Marbell sends a bundle of Jeff's letters to Kate, asking her to forward them to Mary. The "sheaf of . . . thick white envelopes" reawakens Kate's passion for Jeff, and she keeps and eventually reads the letters (267). Mary recoils in horror at the thought of her mother reading Jeff's letters, yet another example of Spencer's interweaving of family and social politics.

fragmentary contact with those she loves, treasuring memories of earlier days in order to sustain her dreams of future reunion. She is, however, not alone in this experience. Jeff, Kathy, Kate, Kate's husband Fred—all the major characters in the novel suffer the stress of loneliness and dislocation.

In this sense, then, the novel's four chapters of dramatic dialogue are perfectly suited to Spencer's theme. These four short chapters (totaling only five full pages of print), appearing approximately half-way through the novel, contrast starkly with the more traditional narrative structures around them. With their frighteningly disembodied voices, Spencer suggests dramatically the profound displacement that individuals must experience when a culture is dissolving from internal conflict. Like the dramatized chapters in *Moby-Dick*, they present apparently unfiltered dialogue, in several instances from quite mysterious characters. They are like the first-person chapters in purpose because they also dramatize the alienation and distance that characterize so much of this world. In the first dramatized chapter (part two, chapter seven), Spencer uses dialogue to portray an encounter between Mary and her psychiatrist, Dr. Skoletsky. The form is appropriate to their distant, cold, unproductive relationship. This same emotional coldness and officious objectivity characterizes all the encounters Spencer chooses for this form. In the second instance (part two, chapter nine), four antiwar activists meeting in secret and identified only by titles such as "First Speaker" and "Second Speaker, a Woman" coldheartedly discuss Jeff's growing insta-bility over Mary's suicide attempt. They casually dismiss her as "not admitted to full confidence" and having "a neurotic weakness in her character," and dissect him as "fit for a lobotomy" (164). While Spencer brilliantly establishes a personality for each of the four voices in less than a page and a half, they are uniformly dedicated to their mission to the exclusion of any individual interest.

By using the form to imply a comparison between a state-appointed psychiatrist and four antiwar reactionaries, Spencer implies that the antiwar movement is Jeff and Mary's enemy just as surely as any other monolithic group. Immediately following the dialogue of the activists comes the third of these chapters. It adds to the gallery of uncaring voices the frightening dinner table conversa-tion at Fred and Kate's Main Line home. After Kate and Fred profess family-oriented generosity to their friends, Spencer adds in italics a quick glimpse inside Kate's mind, revealing her paranoid fantasies about her daughter and granddaughter. The last of the four chapters returns to Mary and Dr. Skoletsky, whose logic Mary says later is like "spiked boots trampling over [her] spread-out feelings," but who convinces her to hold a job for Kathy's sake (169). This second interview is as cold as the first, but it signals a turning point inside Mary, as she begins to seize control of her life while maintaining her allegiance to Jeff and Kathy.

With these dramatized chapters, Gerda Stewart's journal, Mary's recordings, and Jeff's desperate letters, Spencer has written into the text of *The Night Travellers* a litany of loneliness. She obviously intends them to convey dramatically the theme suggested by her plot—that human beings cannot exist in a vacuum. When isolated either physically or emotionally by circumstance, they will use every resource available to maintain or reform threatened relationships. In particular, Spencer argues, they are bound by the need for certain archetypal relationships, such as the ties backward to parents and forward to children and the ties to a permanent mate.

When these relationships are suspended or broken, the characters consciously or unconsciously begin seeking human replacements to fill the void. The novel teems with examples; the makeshift household Mary establishes with Estes Drover, Mary and Jeff's dependency on Ethan Marbell as a second father, and the toddler Kathy's acceptance of a wild Canadian trapper are only the most obvious. In the world of *The Night Travellers* it is impossible to escape the psychological need for certain identifying relationships—except through death.[6] It is no accident, then, that Spencer has Mary refer to a photo in an archaeology text as the image she retains for her own nuclear family. Spencer's message is clear—that the human animal is a communal animal that must form stable, nurturing groups to retain its identity and sanity.

With her carefully crafted fifth section, "Divisions and Dilemmas," Spencer uses this theme to create a suspense that is missing from the end of *The Salt Line*. This and other part titles of the novel—"The Home Scene," "Voices from Afar," "Scatterings," "Reunion"—serve to focus the reader's attention on Jeff and Mary's desperate need for a shared life. In the last section, Spencer plays out the pattern of separation and reunion to a high point of expectancy,

6. In contrast, Martha Ingram of *Knights and Dragons*, published twenty-six years earlier, was able to break free of her disastrous relationship to her husband, but only by erasing the need for human contact of any kind.

writing lyrically of both their mature need each for the other and the grace with which they face this last, most desperate roadblock. Two only children, by the novel's end they have become *twins*, bonded by their suffering and their mutual need. Mary's primal vision of herself "seated by the fire, the child on her lap, [Jeff] just standing . . . to reassure their safety," is at the center of Spencer's vision as well (151), for the figures in the tableau are bound both by desire and necessity, drawing from each other their identity.

Just as the structure of *The Salt Line* echoes Forster's *A Passage to India*, another novel about the possibility/impossibility of human connection, the ending of *The Night Travellers* suggests Forster's closing dictum in *Aspects of the Novel*. Forster, like Spencer, finds fiction's "nearest parallel" in music. On the last page of his chapter on "pattern and rhythm" in fiction, Forster argues that the wise novelist does not strive for a definitive sense of closure but rather for "expansion" at a novel's end: "Not Completion. Not rounding off but opening out." Spencer captures precisely this sense of suspended potential at the end of *The Night Travellers*.[7]

Spencer calls the last brief chapter in the novel "Foreverness," an echo of the phrase that she used earlier in part four, "The ties that bind are holding forever" (323). In a sense this folk saying serves as a fitting reference point to Spencer's entire canon, for, as it illustrates, close human ties *bind* by both nurturing and constraining. Many of Spencer's most interesting characters fight to escape the damaging constraints of unhealthy relationships; many more struggle against all-but-impossible odds to maintain relationships that give them identity and hope. We all desire to escape the ties that bind, Spencer is saying over and over, to know ourselves powerful and independent. But that desire is balanced, she also reminds us, by the need to be known, loved, and shared by some deeply significant others. Her message in *The Night Travellers* is that the ties that doubly bind us are finally dissolved only by death. We are all suspended in a complex web of relationships that we can neither successfully deny nor fully escape. At the end of *The Night Travellers*, Spencer's reader must conclude, like Marilee Summerall at the end of "Sharon," that we all share, "near and powerful," the same "living blood."

7. E. M. Forster, *Aspects of the Novel* (New York, 1927), 168, 169.

Conclusion

It would be manifestly unfair to argue that Spencer's fiction is confined to a single theme. The depth and complexity of her vision support an exploration of a number of issues other than community, several of which are worth mentioning here.

First, Spencer's career illustrates clearly the organic connection between the artist's technical growth and the growth of her understanding. When Spencer abandoned the more traditional narrative forms of *Fire in the Morning* and *The Voice at the Back Door* for the experiments of *Knights and Dragons* and later novels, she did so in order to explore more fully the inner lives of her characters. As her understanding of her characters grew in depth and complexity, her technical skill increased as well. In other words, she discovered what she had to say as she discovered new and better ways of saying it. Any serious study of her fiction will have to take into account its increasingly sophisticated marriage of medium and message.

A second significant issue is Spencer's "southernness." Her first three novels caused critics to label her a traditional southern novelist in the grand tradition of the Southern Renascence. After 1960, however, she evolved into quite a different sort of "southern" writer and did so in a way undetected by most of her critics. I believe that by virtue of her consistent concern with the dynamics of community she should be read as "southern" even when her setting is Italy or Canada. No matter where the story is set, her primary concern is that quintessentially southern one—the individual caught in the communal web. When she came around to setting *The Snare* in New Orleans and *The Salt Line* on the Mississippi Gulf coast, she brought to bear a number of nontraditional techniques on her newly reimagined South. It is time for critics and scholars of southern literature to reacquaint themselves with Spencer, not only as an expatriate abroad but also as a prophet returned.

It is common practice in discussing influences on Spencer to note first Eudora Welty and Henry James. Although both of these comparisons are certainly valid, it will be much harder to prove the influence of James than of Welty. In addition, scholars would do well to attend to the 1990 appreciation of Fielding's *Joseph Andrews* that Spencer published in the *Sewanee Review*.[1] Readers of footnotes will have already deduced my own fascination with the similarities between Spencer's fiction and that of E. M. Forster, another author obsessed with the spirituality of human relations. Spencer is a well-educated (she has an M.A. from Vanderbilt; she did her thesis on Yeats), well-read author, capable of allusion to Dante as well as to Baudelaire in *The Snare* alone. This aspect of her fiction is yet another rich scholarly field waiting to be cultivated.

Finally, the theme of community is, as Spencer has noted, an ancient one with profound religious implications. In *The Snare* (written in the late 1960s), Spencer emphasized the spirituality inherent in her thematic material when she focused on Julia Garrett's intense response to an informal ritual of communion. In *The Salt Line,* she focused on the regenerative power of the Gulf coast, suggesting the spirituality of place, in which she believes quite strongly. These are only two examples, but they serve to suggest a pattern that is there throughout. Because of these spiritual overtones, Spencer's focus on community has served her well in addressing any number of serious issues—from race relations to cultural strife. More important, this spiritual element has raised her fiction above its local place and time to a level of universal significance.

For thirty-five years, Elizabeth Spencer has kept one thematic issue squarely in her artistic sights—the ties that bind individuals together. Even in the earliest stories and novels, that single word *bind* cut with a double edge; examined closely, intimate relations in Spencer's work both sustain and restrain. Depending on their personalities and needs, many important Spencer characters flee all who love them and, like Randall Gibson, all who even know them. The ultimate value of Spencer's long and productive career may well be that she has managed, through the seasons, to sustain this same profound artistic vision, examining ever more closely its texture and implications.

For these and other reasons, Elizabeth Spencer's best work not only demands critical reevaluation but will richly reward any who attempt it. It is high time that scholars and teachers began to heed the many voices she has created, for the stories they tell are deeply significant. These are stories that diagnose our cultural wounds and remind us of the communal ties that can bind them.

1. Elizabeth Spencer, "Another Look at *Joseph Andrews,*" *Sewanee Review,* XCVIII (1990), 668–73.

Bibliography

Adams, Phoebe. Review of *The Light in the Piazza,* by Elizabeth Spencer. *Atlantic Monthly,* CCVII (February, 1961), 113.

Adams, Phoebe-Lou. "Short Reviews." *Atlantic,* CCLIII (February, 1984), 104.

Baker, Carlos. "Two American Marriages." *New York Times Book Review,* October 22, 1967, p. 8.

Bell, Madison Smartt. "A Bond of Braided Histories." *New York Times Book Review,* September 4, 1988, p. 6.

Black, Susan M. "A Dream in Italy." *New Republic,* December 5, 1960, p. 20.

Brinnin, John Malcolm. "Black and White in Redneck Country." *Washington Post Book World,* May 15, 1983, p. 10.

Creekmore, Herbert. "Submerged Antagonisms." *New York Times Book Review,* September 12, 1948, pp. 14–16.

Duvall, John N. *Faulkner's Marginal Couple: Invisible, Outlaw, and Unspeakable Communities.* Arlington, Tex., 1990.

Enright, C. J. "The Landscape of the Heart." *Times Literary Supplement,* July 15, 1983, p. 745.

Evoy, Karen. "Marilee: 'A Permanent Landscape of the Heart.' " *Mississippi Quarterly,* XXXVI (1983), 569–78.

Fairman, H. W. "The Kingship Rituals of Egypt." In *Myth, Ritual, and Kingship,* edited by S. H. Hooke. Oxford, 1958.

Flint, R. W. "Recent Fiction." *Hudson Review,* I (1949), 590.

Forster, E. M. *Aspects of the Novel.* New York, 1927.

————. *A Passage to India.* London, 1924.

Gill, Brendan. "Books: All Praise." *New Yorker,* December 15, 1956, p. 180.

Hicks, Granville. "Lives Like Assorted Pastries." *Saturday Review,* October 21, 1967. pp. 29–30.

Kauffmann, Stanley. "Sense and Sensibility." *New Republic,* June 26, 1965, pp. 27–28.

Melville, Herman. *Moby-Dick.* Boston, 1956.

Nettels, Elsa. "Elizabeth Spencer." In *Southern Women Writers: The New Generation,* edited by Tonette Bond Inge. Tuscaloosa, 1990.

Park, Clara Claiborne. "A Personal Road." *Hudson Review,* XXXIV (1981–82), 601–605.

Prenshaw, Peggy Whitman. *Elizabeth Spencer.* Boston, 1985.

————, ed. *Conversations with Elizabeth Spencer.* Jackson, 1991.

Prescott, Orville. "Books of the Times." *New York Times,* November 21, 1960, p. 27.

————. "Books of the Times: All Aggravation and Ambiguity." *New York Times,* June 30, 1965, p. 35.

Price, Reynolds. "The Art of American Short Stories." *New York Times Book Review,* March 1, 1981, p. 1.

Roberts, Terry. Unpublished interview with Elizabeth Spencer. September 10, 1990.

Rubin, Louis D., Jr. "From Combray to Ithaca: or, The 'Southernness' of Southern Literature." In Rubin, *The Mockingbird in the Gum Tree: A Literary Gallimaufry.* Baton Rouge, 1991.

Spencer, Elizabeth. "Another Look at *Joseph Andrews.*" *Sewanee Review,* XCVIII (1990), 668–73.

————. *Fire in the Morning.* New York, 1948.

————. *Jack of Diamonds.* New York, 1988.

————. *Knights and Dragons.* New York, 1965.

————. Letter to the author, January 26, 1993.

————. *The Light in the Piazza.* New York, 1960.

————. *Marilee.* Jackson, 1981.

————. *The Night Travellers.* New York, 1991.

————. *No Place for an Angel.* New York, 1967.

————. *On the Gulf.* Jackson, 1991.

————. *The Salt Line.* Garden City, N.Y., 1984.

————. *Ship Island and Other Stories.* New York, 1968.

————. *The Snare.* New York, 1972.

————. *The Stories of Elizabeth Spencer.* Garden City, N.Y., 1981.

————. *This Crooked Way.* New York, 1952.

————. *The Voice at the Back Door.* New York, 1956.

Sullivan, Walter. "Fiction in a Dry Season: Some Signs of Hope." *Sewanee Review,* LXXVII (Winter, 1969), 163–64.

Tate, Allen. "The Man of Letters in the Modern World." In Tate, *Collected Essays.* Denver, 1959.

Warren, Robert Penn. " 'The Great Mirage': Conrad and *Nostromo.*" In Warren, *Selected Essays.* New York, 1951.

Woodland, Randy. " 'In That City Foreign and Paradoxical': The Idea of New Orleans in the Southern Literary Imagination." Ph.D. dissertation, University of North Carolina, 1987.

Yeats, William Butler. "Crazy Jane Talks with the Bishop." In Yeats, *The Poems: A New Edition,* edited by Richard J. Finneran. New York, 1983.

Index